Only the Gospel Is Revolutionary

# Only the Gospel Is Revolutionary

*The Church in the Reform of Pope Francis*

ÓSCAR RODRÍGUEZ MARADIAGA

a conversation with Antonio Carriero

translated by Demetrio S. Yocum

LITURGICAL PRESS

Collegeville, Minnesota

www.litpress.org

Originally published as *Solo il Vangelo è Rivoluzionario: La Chiesa di oggi e quella di domani nelle riforme di Francesco* by Piemme © 2017.

**Library of Congress Cataloging-in-Publication Data**

Names: Rodriguez Maradiaga, Oscar Andres, author.
Title: Only the Gospel is revolutionary : the church in the reform of
    Pope Francis / Oscar Rodriguez Maradiaga ; a conversation with
    Antonio Carriero ; translated by Demetrio S. Yocum.
Other titles: Solo il Vangelo e rivoluzionario. English
Description: Collegeville, Minnesota : Liturgical Press, 2018.
Identifiers: LCCN 2017059627 (print) | LCCN 2017043583 (ebook) |
    ISBN 9780814644263 (ebook) | ISBN 9780814644027
Subjects: LCSH: Church renewal—Catholic Church. | Francis, Pope,
    1936–
Classification: LCC BX1746 (print) | LCC BX1746 .R634 2018 (ebook)
    | DDC 282.09/051—dc23
LC record available at https://lccn.loc.gov/2017059627

# CONTENTS

# I

# FROM DON BOSCO TO THE VATICAN

*The Salesian College. Love for Theology.*
*The Gospel and Youth. The Meeting with John Paul II.*

*Who is Óscar Andrés Rodríguez Maradiaga according to . . .*
*Maradiaga?*

I'm a son of Don Bosco. My first encounter with him happened very early in life. I was six years old when my dad took me to the Salesian college where his confessor lived. I was thrilled and excited to see so many children and young people play in the yard.

My father noticed my excitement and told me, "You will come to study here." For me, that was the greatest gift I could receive. The following year I was already in elementary school and the college became my second home.

Not long ago, I met the ambassador of Colombia to the Holy See, who was a Salesian and a student of philosophy, then abandoned the Salesian congregation and went to Germany to pursue a doctorate in philosophy. We talked about the family spirit that you experience with the Salesians. And he told me: "The Salesian house was our family." We both had our parents, sisters, brothers at home . . . but for us, the house was the Salesian school.

There was music and playtime; there were colors, there were the "companies," the ancient formula of modern associations. There, I felt really good with my friends to the point that our superiors had to ask us to return home because we did not want to leave. The family spirit was an essential component of our lives there.

The Salesian director I had from my fourth grade to the penultimate year was for me like Don Bosco. He later became an archbishop. Another Salesian—a German, a strong man to whom I will be forever grateful—was the one who made me fall in love with chemistry and physics so ardently that many years later I decided to study both subjects and then teach them in turn to new generations of students.

*Does the red robe you wear as cardinal perhaps remind you of the one you used to wear as an altar boy?*

That's right. What I wore for the first time at eight years old was the "small clergy" cassock and surplice with which we served at the altar. As an altar boy, I had to get up at 5 a.m., and without having any breakfast, because then we used to fast from midnight until after Holy Communion. I went to church. I would put on my cassock and serve at Mass, which was in Latin and which, to tell the truth, I did not understand much then. We would then recite the rosary and listen to some catechist lessons. Then I would run to breakfast, and at 7:30 I was in class.

Sometimes the school director, who later became my archbishop, would take me to serve Mass with him at the school run by the nuns. We boys would vie with each other to go because it was the only way we could see the girls. One time, on our way back, he asked if I would have liked to become a priest. I immediately replied "yes."

I spoke to my mom about it, but she started to cry and told me that I was still too young to decide, that my health was not perfect, and that I should have asked for my father's permission. He in turn told me that I was too naughty to become a priest and that surely they would expel me the day after joining the seminary. And in any case, he said, I could decide only after completing high school.

I took it very badly. It was a real disappointment for me. I put my dream aside and decided to become a pilot instead, as some of my other relatives. I liked flying and I used to feed this other passion of mine by reading aviation books; studying English, the language of pilots; drawing airplanes, and transforming them into models.

*You cultivate two important "passions": science and music. How did they enter your life?*

The former was instilled in me by a Salesian priest, a real genius. The latter came from my family. My dad, coming home from work, would always put on some music, while my older sister was a pianist. Soon I started to strum on something myself. So my father enrolled me at the local music school. I endured there only two or three months, because I couldn't stand the idea that on Saturday afternoons while I was practicing *solfeggio* my siblings were out playing. Fortunately, a young Spanish Salesian who played the accordion very well arrived at our college. I was fourteen years old, and I fell in love with that instrument right away. The following year that Salesian was transferred, and I continued on my own.

*At the end of high school, did you take up again the subject of your vocation, left open years earlier, with your father?*

We were in the middle of January 1960. I went to my father and asked him: "Do you remember the promise you made about me becoming a priest?" There was no need for many words. He took me by car, with my suitcase and accordion, and we arrived at the Salesian house where I entered the novitiate. I chose them because I longed to teach and become an educator. And the Salesians specialize in that field.

*Was there really nothing that you did not like of the Salesians?*

One thing that struck me was that the priests were moved from one country to another, from one house to the other, without much explanation given to us, or almost without saying anything, until the new school year began. I saw how the priests, the clerics, the coadjutor brothers were transferred to other states, and this seemed very tough, even cruel to us since we were on friendly terms and had learned to respect them. Only later did I learn that it was because in consecrated life they took a vow of obedience and that according to this principle they always had to be ready to go wherever it was necessary. To me, it seemed pure madness to have to leave my country and family and go away. But in due time I understood, and I myself have experienced, in my Salesian life, the moment of being always ready to go and obey.

*What was instead the aspect that fascinated you the most of the Salesian charism?*

Joy, the quality of its community life. Above all, I was struck by the fact that there were Salesians of so many nationalities and that, nonetheless, they worked together on a single project, and that everyone followed Don Bosco's teachings with love.

My province, or the Salesian district to which I belong, is that of Central America and is composed of confreres of six different nations; this extraordinary variety also included the missionary confreres coming from Austria, Germany, Italy, Hungary, Spain, etc. Yet we were united, happily working and living together.

That exuberance of joy made us fall in love with the Gospel and the Salesian ideal. We would spend all day at the Salesian house, until they would tell us to go back to our homes at sunset, and we would go with great sadness and with the desire to return the next day.

*After studying philosophy and theology, did you realize your dream of becoming a teacher?*

I was asked to teach theology in the morning, in the same institute where I studied the year before, and in the afternoon chemistry at a Salesian high school. One day, however, my superior (whom we Salesians call "director") called me and proposed that I go study canon law in Rome. I said, "Please, no. I'm still figuring things out and you want to groom me already." We talked for a long time, and in the end I was happy to be sent to study moral theology instead.

That is how I began studying at the Alphonsianum in Rome. One fine day, the professor of morals and psychology, an Austrian Redemptorist father, asked me and five other students if we felt like adding another study subject along with moral theology. We accepted. It was a clinical psychology course at the Sapienza University on Saturdays, and in the summer we would continue in Austria, at Innsbruck. So, after completing the studies of moral theology, I also found myself with a diploma in clinical psychology. I returned to Guatemala with these titles and I was appointed director of the seminary, until I received a phone call from the Nunciature where they said to me: "The nuncio would like to see you on Monday at nine." I had a problem with the cardinal of Guatemala: his seminarians studied in our seminary, and the diocese had to pay tuition, but he did not want to pay. So, after the call from the nuncio I said to my accountant: "Please prepare for me a report of all the expenses to prove to the nuncio that we need that money, because I imagine that the cardinal went to talk to the nuncio to create problems." The poor bookkeeper spent the weekend figuring out the numbers.

*What happened then when you went to the Nuncio?*

I arrived that Monday at the Nunciature already prepared for battle, when a nun saw me and said: "Are you the priest who has an appointment with Monsignor Higuera?" Ah! It was not the nuncio to Guatemala, but the nuncio to Honduras! "What's going on?" I was quite alarmed. The nuncio finally came in and said to me, "Father, I duped you." "No," I replied, "because the nun just told me that the appointment was with you." Then the nuncio smiled at me and said: "Now you understand why nuns cannot be priests? They can't keep secrets!"

After laughing together, he asked for an opinion on a Honduran priest who was a candidate to become bishop. I thought to myself, "Aren't these consultations made in writing; what was the need to have me come here from another country?" But I answered his question. I confessed that I did not know that priest well, but I also told him what I thought of him. After that, the nuncio told me: "What would you say if the Holy Father called you to serve in Honduras?" I promptly replied: "I do not think it will happen because I work at a seminary, and we Salesians have no seminaries in Honduras." "No," replied the nuncio, "it is not for that, but as a bishop." At that point, I almost thought I was facing death. I was thirty-five years old; it would have been unimaginable. I'm sorry, your excellency, but that is not my vocation. My vocation is to be a Salesian. Can't you find someone else?" And the nuncio said: "You must give me an answer." And I: "I cannot right now. I need to pray and talk about it with my confessor." Then he concluded: "All right; we will meet again on Easter Monday, in Tegucigalpa, and you will give me your final answer."

*Was it a painful choice? In other words, you had always been with your students.*

That Lent I felt miserable. For me it was almost a death sentence. But I prayed a lot, and the next day I consulted with my confessor, my spiritual director. I did not know what to say to my director. I should have told him: "I have to go to Honduras, but I cannot tell you why." He laughed. I later understood why: he had already been consulted well in advance. I went to the Nunciature convinced in all conscience that I should say no after consulting with my confessor and so much prayer. In the office of the nuncio, I did not have the time to say a word: "Before answering my question, read this letter." It was Paul VI who asked me to accept for the good of the Honduran church. At that point, what could I say? I remembered Don Bosco saying, "A Pope's wish is an order for a Salesian." In Spanish it is said *"Fui por lana y volví trasquilado"*—"I went for wool and came back shorn." So I became bishop against my wish, without knowing anything and without pastoral preparation. But I was also defiant, for I had objected to the nuncio: "I am in the middle of the school year. How can I leave? There is no one to replace me. Let us talk about it again in October." It was the only concession he made.

Later, on August 6, we were at a meeting of the provincial council of our Salesian province, in San Salvador, when the news came that Paul VI had died. My goodness! I remember thinking, "My God, set me free." John Paul I was soon elected; he confirmed my appointment and died one month later. I then prayed again: "Lord, please . . . let me be," but it was left unanswered. On October 22, 1978, John Paul II became pope, and six days later I was appointed bishop. Mine was one of his first appointments. The relationship that binds me to him runs very deep.

*Was it easy for you to obey the many requests of your superiors?*

After high school, my Salesian superiors admitted me to aspirancy, which lasted five months, because I wanted to become a Salesian as well. And there, during that time, I studied Latin and Greek.

During the last month, my superior came to tell me: "Here you are wasting your time. I'll send you to our novitiate." So, one evening, the superior gave the announcement that I would go to the novitiate. All the other aspirants were sad. "You will lose your vocation . . ." someone said to me, but the superior snapped back saying that I would join the novitiate. End of story. Everyone laughed. I joined the novitiate with other mates.

In 1961—the year in which I took final vows—I went to college to study philosophy. In the first year, almost all subjects corresponded to the last year of secondary school, so I was studying philosophy and continued with Latin and Greek, and in the end I finished the first year of philosophy in four months. In the second year, I studied pedagogy and magisterial teaching, and after the second year my superior informed me that I would take an internship, and I was sent to teach fifth and sixth graders in the aspirantate. I was also the choir master and orchestra director, as I took on several other tasks. It was a great year.

I was preparing a Christmas show when my superior came and took me by the arm. We all knew that when he took someone by the arm it meant a new assignment. "How are you doing?" he asked, and I said, "Fine! I'm preparing a Christmas recital." And he: "Tomorrow you will have to go to Sant'Anna as a professor of chemistry and music." I prepared my suitcase and the next day I was in Sant'Anna.

That obedience cost me a lot. There, however, I spent two years of apprenticeship just as valuable, to the point that I did not want to go to study theology and leave that place behind. When I completed my studies and had already been ordained—because we took holy orders in June and the academic year ended in October (this was a beautiful tradition that no longer exists: in fact, it is better to be ordained during the last year of studies, so during the second semester, and already a priest, one can still consult with the superiors of the theologate)—I asked my superior: "And now?" And he said to me: "Go home for a while, for a vacation, then I'll let you know." So I went on vacation and one day I got a phone call from my superior: "Óscar, are you ready?" And I: "Yes, of course." "You will go back the theologate as a teacher." "Is that a joke?" I replied, "Until last year I was one of them, and now you want me to return as their superior? I don't like this." And the superior: "You will go!" All right. In the end, I obeyed.

I stayed there for two years, teaching also ecclesiology, chemistry in the afternoon, and in the evening ecclesiology at the institute of the sisters. Saturday and Sunday I was in the oratory. I was very happy.

After studying moral theology, I left Sant'Anna and returned as director of studies of the theologate. And after four months the new superior came and said to me: "Tomorrow you will go as new director to the philosophate." How was that possible? I was only thirty years old. How would I manage? I obeyed. It was my penultimate obedience because the last one was not to the Salesian congregation, but to the pope himself, as I accepted to become auxiliary bishop of Tegucigalpa.

*Let's go back to your episcopal ordination. Were you ordained on a special day? And how did you learn to be a bishop?*

It was December 8, a date I chose because it is the foundation date of the Salesian congregation and the feast of the Immaculate Conception of Mary. I was consecrated by the apostolic nuncio, Archbishop Gabriel Montalvo Higuera, my archbishop Héctor Enrique Santos Hernández, and another Salesian archbishop who would later become Cardinal Miguel Obando Brando of Nicaragua and who was my director during the years of practical internship. So I come from a Salesian lineage.

Two months after my episcopal ordination, the Puebla Conference was held. There were four bishops of Honduras at that time. Two of them went to the conference while I was in the diocese and learned how to be a bishop. A month later, I saw a notice about a course for priests (140 priests!) to study the Puebla document, and I asked the archbishop: "Who will go from Honduras?" "No one," he replied. This was unacceptable, I thought to myself, because the Puebla Conference represented a turning point in the pastoral needs of Latin America, so I asked to go and the archbishop gave me his permission. I found out that at that course we were only three bishops, all the others were priests; with me I had brought two priests and two lay men. It lasted nine weeks, and I still consider that period as a true spiritual exercise: we studied the Puebla document passionately. For me, that experience was the beginning of my episcopate. When we returned to our diocese, our team had the task of visiting all the cities of the diocese to implement and make known the Puebla Document. It was a very rewarding experience.

Afterward, they nominated me secretary of the conference and then delegate to CELAM, the Latin American Bishops' Conference. CELAM was a true school for my ministry: I started as a member of the Department of Education, and two years later I was appointed president of the Youth Department, and then later also president of the Department for Consecrated Life, secretary general, finance manager, president—for a total of twenty-four years of service at CELAM, during which I was able to meet almost all of the 1,200 bishops of Latin America because I had to go to the conference meetings. I was among those who organized the Santo Domingo Conference, which was the fourth general conference of the Latin American bishops, and then a few years later I worked with then-Cardinal Bergoglio, who at the Aparecida Conference was the chairman of the committee charged with drafting the final document, of which I was also a member. I still remember the many hours spent discussing, writing, correcting, and rewriting the famous Aparecida Document.

I have also been an apostolic administrator in a diocese in the west of the country. The apostolic nuncio told me to go there for only three months to prepare the succession, and those three months became three years. It was a very difficult period, because it was the period of the guerrilla crisis in Guatemala and El Salvador, and we had twenty thousand refugees packed in what looked like concentration camps. The army considered me the head of the opposition movement. Can you imagine a simple man like me as the leader of any subversion?

When I was secretary general of CELAM, I had to go to Colombia for four years and live in Bogotá, where we also attacked by the guerrillas, and I had to act as a mediator. After all these adventures, on January 8, 1993, I was appointed archbishop of Tegucigalpa.

*After so many important assignments in Latin America you were . . . called by the Vatican.*

True, the Vatican has never left me in peace. I was first named "consultor for clergy," then a member of "Cor Unum" where I stayed four years. I also worked at the Pontifical Council for Justice and Peace, which no longer exists, for twenty years, and then I became a member of the Pontifical Council for Social Communications until that dicastery was closed; and I was secretary of the Synod and member of the Latin American Commission. I certainly did not have time to get bored. When I thought I had already given enough, Pope Francis, in 2013, appointed me coordinator of the "Council of Nine" in charge of assisting the pope in the task of reforming the government of the church and the Roman Curia.

*You said that your relationship with John Paul II was very special. What joyful memories do you keep of the pope who made you a cardinal of the Holy Roman Church?*

There are many. The first time we met was in Brazil, in 1980. Pope John Paul II came for CELAM's twenty-fifth anniversary. I was the delegate for my diocese, but I had been bishop for just a year and a half, so when I introduced myself to him he welcomed me as a son. I was thirty-six years old. He asked, "Can you sing?" and I replied: "Yes, Your Holiness. What do you want me to sing?" And he said, " 'The Fisherman'!" And so I sang that song.

That meeting for us was sad because an epidemic of highly contagious influenza exploded, and the contagion spread from the famous Maracanã stadium because out of nowhere came this incredible cold front, when usually in Rio de Janeiro the climate is tropical and hot. The next day I had a very high fever and could not get up. So I have only a few memories of the pope's visit in 1980.

The second occasion was in 1983, during my first *ad limina* visit, when I was apostolic administrator of the Diocese of Santa Rosa de Copán, Honduras. It was a beautiful hearing. When I entered the room, the pope had the map of Honduras on the table: "Ah, here is a young bishop who has a lot of work to do. So, tell me about the refugee situation." At that time, we were hosting twenty thousand refugees from El Salvador, in temporary accommodation centers; the diocese experienced tremendous difficulties. The army thought we were revolutionaries, because the great majority of the refugees were the wives and sons of the guerrillas. But they were simply poor people whom we could not abandon. That *ad limina* visit was very special as John Paul II listened to me with great care, but he also found a way to lighten the atmosphere with a little humor. At that time I was very young, and so he asked me, smiling: "Have you made your first Communion yet?"

*How did your meetings with him take place at the Vatican?*

After being elected CELAM's secretary general, once a year I would go to meet the Holy Father at the Vatican. He would always say to me: "No hearings, let's have lunch together instead." Then I would call Bishop Stanislaw, the pope's secretary, who would then tell me the day I would have to come and have lunch with the Holy Father. It was great how John Paul II talked to me while joking around. He would also ask me many questions. Sometimes our lunches would last for about two hours. We would always go first to the Blessed Sacrament in the chapel and end our meeting in prayer.

One time I had to meet the pope for a very serious matter regarding Latin America, and I asked if he could meet me but without my visit being reported to the *Osservatore Romano*—so he invited me to dinner. I arrived on time for dinner and I remember that I waited in a waiting room; I heard his steps approaching, and when he came in he took my hands and said, "Let's go and pray so you can tell me all you have to say." The dinner was great, but the pope was saddened. He told me: "Nobody has informed me of these things, so thank you for letting me know." And then, at the end of another visit, after praying in front of the Blessed Sacrament, I asked the pope: "Your Holiness, please, I ask for a prayer for tomorrow as I will celebrate eleven years as bishop," and he replied: "Is that your eleventh birthday as well?" He was always joking with me.

Once we were at lunch and I asked him, "Holiness, when are you coming to Cuba?" He looked at me and said: "Well, when CELAM organizes a visit," and so we immediately prepared it, and in every detail. He was always very close to us CELAM bishops; he was of great support, even when there was a war in Santo Domingo that wanted CELAM to disappear, and he prevented it. For me, John Paul II's visits always provided a great stimulus for pastoral care, for his holiness was palpable.

I also witnessed some miracles he performed during his life. Once I took some documents on Wojtyła's miracles (those I myself saw and those witnessed by others) to Bishop Stanislaw and he cried saying, "These things also happen here often, but we cannot say anything to the pope because he does not give them too much importance. We will keep these documents for the future."

His memory is still alive in me. John Paul II was a reserved person; he was less extroverted than Pope Francis, who is more expansive. I remember, however, that John Paul II one day hugged me, and he was certainly not the hugging type, as his Polish culture is more reserved.

*Your Eminence, how do you know so many different languages?*

I was lucky with languages. In the Salesian College, during high school, we studied a year of Latin, three years of French, and five years of English. In those years I learned the basics, which I then perfected during my novitiate year. There I also learned Italian, the "official language" we all had to know. I also practiced by reading a famous comic book, *Il Vittorioso* (The Winner), and listening to Italian songs. I remember that with my fellow theology students we performed the Sanremo songs with the orchestra I had put on at the Italian Cultural Center of Guatemala. In those days the songs of the "festival of the flowers" were beautiful, not like those of today. People loved to hear the seminarians sing in Italian. I can say that I have enjoyed Salesian life intensely and continue to live as Salesian even today, as happy as I can ever be.

*Do you still like to be called "Salesian of Don Bosco"? Considering that the pastoral responsibilities you assumed as bishop and then as cardinal have forced you to stay away from young people?*

What a great question! As a matter of fact, I am Salesian by vocation and bishop by obedience, as I was snatched from Don Bosco's ranks to serve in the church as bishop. At thirty-six, I was consecrated auxiliary bishop of Tegucigalpa, where I worked with another Salesian, the late Monsignor Héctor Enrique Santos, who was my "mentor." Therefore, I was not born a bishop, but I learned step by step—and I am still learning. I always sign S.D.B., which stands for "Salesian of Don Bosco," just to remember my identity because, as Pope Francis put it so well, we must not forget who we are and where we come from. My story has been shaped by so many elements and details that have created the fabric of my life. I am fortunate to serve the church in a country where young people are the majority of the population, and for this reason I feel Salesian.

*Do you think Don Bosco is still relevant today?*

Don Bosco is always relevant because he founded the Salesians to educate poor and abandoned youth. Unfortunately, poor youngsters are everywhere, and education—especially public education—is inadequate, which is not to say useless. That is why we are just as relevant as in Don Bosco's time. Alas, there are many places in the world where so many diocesan priests are not at all interested in young people. Some have given up even before starting the battle, by thinking that they are a lost cause and there is nothing left to do; others are scared, or do not know how to deal with them.

Don Bosco is a saint beloved by everybody around the world. Panama, for example, is a unique country for its devotion for Don Bosco, and its history is fascinating. At the beginning of the twentieth century, when the Panama Canal was being built, there were so many workers and many orphans due to an epidemic of yellow fever. There was an Italian Salesian, Fr. Domenico Soldati, who had been sent from Chile to Panama. And what did he find there? So many orphaned children because of the epidemic. Thus, he opened a small hospice for orphans. Later on, he founded a technical school where almost all the workers in Panama learned a craft. Don Bosco is part of the Panamanians' soul.

Each year, on the occasion of Don Bosco's feast, on January 31, we pray three novenas daily for nine days until January 31: one at five in the morning, one at half past six, and the other at seven; then throughout the day the basilica remains open for confessions. There are even people who go to their "Easter" confession (i.e. once a year) on the feast of Don Bosco!

I have been invited a dozen times to preach those novenas. It is a huge effort, because the climate is hot and humid, so when about 1,200 people come every day to church, you are exhausted at the end of the day. On his feast day there is a procession of about 400,000 people, and the city is literally paralyzed. Not even in Turin is it like this. Now in Panama there is also a relic of Don Bosco that the rector major of the Salesians decided to donate to this land.

Young people are waiting for us. We Salesians are not out of fashion. We are very relevant today. Unfortunately, we have to convince many Salesian confreres of this, as they think they are already "retired." But this is what the world wants now—to work less and less. Instead Don Bosco recommended for us work and more work—and we cannot forget that.

*What do young people seek in adults today?*

For me, one of the problems is their confusion. We have advanced technologies to guide us—for example, GPS, which allows one to reach any place in the world, but we lack a "spiritual GPS." So many young people are empty inside and do not know God, because no one has spoken to them, and they seek but cannot find. I think this is a problem. Another point is that many adults say that these young people are good for nothing, so they keep away from them. Then, in many families they have forgotten what the word "young" means, because they are no longer children, and this is a social problem. That is why we need a church that "goes forth."

We must leave our sacristies behind and go in search of young people, finding them where they are, without waiting for them to come to us. Young people want us to be their friends, to be with them, in the midst of them, not to condemn them but to be friends. And that is plain and simple. At my age I have no problem starting a new relationship with the younger generations. If I start singing, they all sing and are happy, and then we can talk.

*So, as a shepherd of a vast flock, you never stopped looking for ways to approach young people?*

Definitely. I have beautiful memories of the World Youth Days with them, doing catechesis and attending their events. In my diocese, on Saturdays before Palm Sunday I meet many young people. And I do not miss this meeting with them even if I break a tooth, as it once happened. I had to run to the dentist, who made an emergency repair, but then I came back to meet with them. There were about 3,500 waiting for catechesis, and I could not disappoint them saying "My tooth just broke." With my mouth a bit swollen because of the sedation and with a bit of fatigue, of course, I managed to continue with the catechesis. It was beautiful, as always, because young people are of God. Another opportunity I never let go by is to administer confirmation. On average I administer it to 10,000 a year. And this, too, is a great joy for me.

# II

# A PASTOR IN LATIN AMERICA

## *Liberation Theology. Political Corruption.*
## *The Fight against Drug Trafficking.*

*Your diocese is vast. How do you visit it from one extreme to the other?*

Yes, my diocese in Honduras is 23,000 square kilometers. The southernmost parish is six and a half hours by car, with terrible road conditions. By helicopter, I am there in forty minutes. I have a pilot's license, so in a single day I can do what otherwise I would do in three days. I have so many ex-students who love me and some of them have helicopters, so I take advantage of that. Even the state aviation, which has made me an honorary commander, sometimes gives me a ride. But I do not make the most of that, although many are good friends.

*A helicopter pilot and "pilot" of a vast Honduran diocese. How do you like to address your flock?*

I like to introduce myself as a "father"—I am the father-bishop of a very complex and populous diocese.

As the archbishop of the capital of the republic of Honduras, I am inevitably involved in national dynamics. I focus more, however, on my pastoral work and on the many activities that are needed to guide, animate, govern, and sanctify a diocese. But I can also count on the help of an auxiliary bishop, a team of episcopal vicars, who give me a hand in my missionary work, and the competence of a special secretary whom the Salesian congregation has granted me. My people are mostly very simple; they bear the deep scars of poverty and pain, and they ask their pastors for closeness, friendship, and paternal love. A flock that is aware of the sincere closeness and sincerity from its bishop is more willing to listen to him.

*What difficulties does the church encounter in Latin America today?*

I think that, as far as priests are concerned, there is a great vocational fragility that can be overcome with a spiritual life that is nourished by faith and profound prayer. The temptation to do many things leads to activism, which erodes and deprives the life of the pastor of meaning. The ideological tendencies seem to have become less relevant in Latin America. The problem today is that of identity, which brings with it the crisis of meaning and vocation. When it comes to the laity, I find that in some environments clericalism is still very strong as a mentality. Finding no opposition, it has allowed and favored the abuse of authority and the maneuvers of certain clerical personalities regarding how to manage parishes and interact within groups, movements, and lay associations.

I believe that many pastoral problems have been very clearly identified by the Fifth General Conference of Latin American Bishops at Aparecida. At that time, they even came up with a good diagnosis. It seems to me that every issue in itself is a challenge that refers to the process we call "New Evangelization" and to which we try to respond with all the apostolic fire we are capable of with the "Continental Mission."

*What can the church of Latin America say to the increasingly de-Christianized Europe?*

As Europe shuts down churches and monasteries, new parishes, dioceses, apostolic vicariates, and missions are emerging in the Americas; orders and religious congregations create new realities. The positive attitude of Latin America in contrast to anti-demographic policies and birth control allows us to believe that the future of the church is in the youth and the redemption of the poor, while without younger generations the future of Europe is compromised.

*Liberation theology in Latin America—where is it mistaken, and what good is there in it? Is it an outdated current of thought?*

Liberation theology is not univocal; it has had several currents. The misunderstanding came from the fact that it tried to use a Marxist analysis of reality as a working tool, and this led some people from the Latin American continent to believe that armed struggle was necessary to defeat poverty. This has caused many deaths and pain in so many countries. But it also brought good things, especially what one of the founders, Fr. Gustavo Gutiérrez, once said: 80 percent of liberation theology is about the preferential option for the poor. This idea has inspired in all countries a more active and social pastoral outreach.

Another positive aspect is the growth of base ecclesial communities, which work pretty well, once they overcome the temptation to be just another political group. These communities have been able to express a greater closeness of pastors to the people, greater ease of life, and a liturgy more incarnate in reality. These can no doubt be considered signs of hope. Liberation theology as a current of thought today is less influential, but the positive fruits remain.

*What is the current political situation in Latin America?*

Unfortunately, there is no political initiative. This is a problem because, after so much corruption—the real evil that has destroyed Latin America—after so many years of military dictatorship, a democracy has emerged, which was renewed in the 1980s, in the sense that elections are held every now and then to elect presidents. However, the idea of conceiving politics as a business—that is, as an opportunity to enrich and spend the rest of one's days without working—has remained. This is one of the biggest evils in political projects.

Then came the drug trafficking that infiltrated politics with a huge influx of money, enriching so many people who closed their eyes so the drugs could pass through. Then came the chavista project,[1] which in the late nineties was a project called "twentieth-century socialism," and it attracted so many people. After fifteen years, however, it proved to be a total failure because it had nothing to do with socialism, but rather it was a form of capitalism for those few who enriched themselves with the state's property. And it was not a twenty-first-century movement but a late nineteenth-century one because that is when Marxism emerged. This project was intended—according to them—to help the poor. True, they did some good things for the poor in Venezuela, but they have also depleted the country, and now they have no food, no medicine, and no freedom. Venezuela is a devastated country—and not long ago it was one of the richest countries in Latin America. That project was a total failure. It was also intended to change the Constitution to have the president reelected without an expiration of his or her term, thus a democratic dictatorship: the goal was to come to power through a democratic process but only to install a dictatorship. This same happened in Ecuador, Bolivia, Nicaragua, and now it is happening in Venezuela. They wanted to do the same in Brazil, but the plan failed. Even in Argentina it failed. So at present there is no political project. What to do?

In my opinion, what is missing is a political education of the younger generations: we must give back to politics its dignity, presenting it as a service to the common good and not as a bargain for a few that impoverishes the entire country. And this has

[1]The political ideology named after Hugo Chávez, president of Venezuela from 1999 to 2013.

not been accomplished yet. How to make it happen? If we Christians start addressing social issues, we are targeted by critics; they say that the Salesians are selling their ideology and are promoting communism. The church's social doctrine is loved and praised by all, but when it comes to practical matters, then resistance comes to light. So we are faced with a great challenge—namely, how to recover true democracy. And then there is so much social injustice, so much inequality, and this is another very serious problem.

*What was the most critical period for you? I mean during the years when you were persecuted by your country's government.*

In 2003, there was a constitutional crisis in Honduras. I was president of the Bishops' Conference when they arrested President Zelaya, forcing him to resign. That was not a coup d'état, but a democratic replacement as the Constitution says. That gentleman wanted to change the Constitution, especially those articles that could not be modified. He wanted to follow in Chávez's footsteps, and then the Republic's Congress deposed him, but a mistake was made in the process: the soldiers put him on a flight to Costa Rica. At that time, the Episcopal Conference published a statement intended only to avoid violence, because the confrontation was very heated and we were afraid of a bloody revolt. I read it when I was president of the Bishops' Conference. So, from that moment on, I was accused of being a *golpista* (coup plotter). Then I was persecuted for denouncing drug traffickers, as that was unthinkable at that time. Now, no more, thank God, but I had a lot of problems for that, and I was also attacked twice; but thank God I keep going, without fear.

# III

# BENEDICT XVI'S RESIGNATION

*The Vatileaks Scandal. The Conclave Debate.*
*The IOR Scandal.*

*Were you also present at the consistory of February 11, 2013, when*
*Benedict XVI shocked everyone announcing his resignation as pope?*

When Benedict XVI made the announcement I was in my
country, meeting with the other bishops of our conference.
Phone calls began: "Do you know what happened?" My goodness! I was also flabbergasted because the previous year we
had had a beautiful visit of the pope in Cuba and Mexico
(where he fell, injuring his head, which caused a lot of bleed-
ing). Nothing, however, prepared us for this. Then there was
that sad Vatileaks case, which certainly caused a great deal of
pain to Benedict. And then came the World Meeting of Families in Milan. I was present and saw the Holy Father closely.
After Mass, I was invited to lunch at the bishop's residence in
Milan. There I saw the pope and he was very depressed. Then
I asked Cardinal Dziwisz, former secretary of John Paul II,
who was next to me, about the butler Paolo Gabriele, who
later turned out to be the "crow": "But where did you find a
guy like that?" He replied that after the resignation of Angelo
Ruggeri they had noticed this young man, very pious, who
first came into service as a cleaning staff member. They often
found him in the chapel praying. "I thought he was a good

man and capable of accompanying the Holy Father." I also think that he was a pious man. Sometimes, however, money ruins people. This might have been another reason for Benedict's depression. I began to pray for him and thought to myself, "My God, what are we going to do with the Holy Father who is so depressed? With a situation like this, you no longer know whom to trust."

*Benedict XVI's decision at the beginning was not understood by all.*

The news of his resignation was a blow to us all. The next morning I got up at 3 a.m., because of the eight-hour difference, to call Cardinal Bertone, then secretary of state, to ask him to explain the pope's decision. "Yes, the Holy Father had to resign," Bertone confirmed on the other end of the phone. "But no, this is impossible," I replied. He continued: "If he does not feel like he can go on, and no longer has the strength, then what can we do? The Holy Father wants us all in Rome before leaving, and then on March 1 we will start the pre-conclave meetings." So I immediately tried to book a flight to come to Italy. Certainly it was a painful decision for Benedict XVI. But I am convinced that the Holy Spirit guided him being the saint that he is. However, not everyone took his renunciation so well. It did not go well with Cardinal Dziwisz, who said that John Paul II, to whom he had been a special secretary, had never come down from the cross. In my opinion, neither did Benedict XVI. He continued, in fact, to carry the cross despite the fact that he had been so vehemently criticized. But with this decision, in my opinion, he opened the door to a more humane future for popes. Just think of Leo XIII, who was almost mentally incapacitated when he died. No one knew because there was no television. But those were different times. Now it is more humane to know that if I do not feel I can go on, if my health does not allow me to go any further, I can give way to a new pope. I think that Benedict XVI has left us a great sign of humility and holiness.

*When you found out about Benedict XVI's resignation, what did you think?*

I thought something serious was happening at the Vatican. At that moment, I put myself in the pope's shoes. I thought he was suffering a lot, but at the same time that his was a brave gesture. Of course, it did not take long to hear all sorts of comments. It was the pope himself who revealed the reasons for his resignation, saying that he was not a king abdicating his throne, but a shepherd who watches out for the good of his sheep and is aware of his limits in being able to serve and defend them. I think the pope has taught us an important lesson here: in public life it is good to retire at the right time. As Miguel de Cervantes wrote in his *Don Quixote*: "To retire is not to flee, and there is no wisdom in waiting when danger outweighs hope."

*At general congregations, cardinals offer speeches intended to identify the most important characteristics that are needed in the new pope. What did you have to say on the topic?*

Some cardinals shared their speeches with reporters. I remember that I called for an end to the practice of *promoveatur ut amoveatur*—that is, getting rid of someone who is a problem by promoting him to another position, which was a very common practice. Then I urged more transparency at the IOR [Istituto per le Opere di Religione; Institute for the Works of Religion], because we were in the middle of the first Vatileaks scandal—a terrible blow, with its many leaks to the press—and then I asked, "Tell us clearly whether the IOR is a bank or not." They told us it was a foundation, but many of their arguments were shaky.

During the general congregations before the conclave, many of the other cardinals were on my side. And I think that precisely from those reflections emerged the so-called Council of the Eight Cardinals (C8)—set up by Pope Francis a few days before the start of his pontificate—with the task to advise him on how to govern the universal church and to work on a draft revision of the apostolic constitution *Pastor bonus* on the Roman Curia.

External observers have said that the church today has a sort of council of ministers, but it actually is an advisory body that was already provided for by the Second Vatican Council, but had never been put into practice before.

The meetings of the C8 now regularly involve the secretary of state, Cardinal Pietro Parolin, so it is possible to speak of a "C9," an unofficial journalistic definition, which, however, is now in current use.

*Why does the IOR exist? People wonder: Why does the Vatican have a bank?*

The IOR is not a bank because it was created as a foundation and it continues as such. The Institute for the Works of Religion is a pontifical private institute created in 1942 by Pope Pius XII and based in Vatican City. It is often mistakenly considered the central bank of the Holy See, a task carried out instead by the Administration of the Patrimony of the Apostolic See (APSA). By statute, its role is "to provide for the safekeeping and administration of movable and immovable property transferred or entrusted to it by physical or juridical persons and intended for works of religion or charity."

Its general manager reports directly to a board of directors consisting of cardinals who in turn respond to the pope.

The IOR has often been involved in financial and nonfinancial scandals. The Institute has therefore launched a new strategy to make its structures and regulations more transparent and put an end to illicit practices.

But I must point out that the Vatican is a state, and an independent state must have a monetary policy and a fund management to operate and maintain its autonomy.

The IOR started, therefore, as a foundation to preserve the assets of religious congregations during World War II. It was carefully created by Pius XII to protect the church's properties in the face of the threat that Hitler might win the war and seize them.

It cannot be denied that in time it became almost a bank and that it also held accounts for people who were not entitled to them. But it was not a big bank; in the list of all the banks in Italy, the IOR occupied the third-to-the-last place. The trouble is that, for example, there were people who wanted to "launder" their money through church accounts by recycling dirty money or by tax evasion. Now everything is in order and clean; the religious congregations and the people who work at the Vatican are the only ones who are allowed to have accounts at the IOR— and that's it! Enough with entrepreneurs who had their money in Switzerland and wanted to bring them here without paying taxes. That game is already over: the economic reform has gone very well, and it continues. We are not finished yet, however. There is still a lot to do, but we are moving forward.

Money is needed. The Vatican Radio, for instance, has a staff of 356 people. How can a company work without money? There was a deficit of about twenty-six million every year. Now the reform has been carried out, but the Holy Father, with great sense of social justice, said: "I do not want these people out on the street without a job." The number of employees, however, should be reduced. If there is someone who is paid but does not do his job, that person can go; but those who work and do their job, those remain. How? As Francis said: "For those who remain, one will think of training them for another job" always within the Curia. That is a good thing.

*What was the atmosphere at the general congregations before the conclave?*

It was a very interesting pre-conclave compared to the first one I attended. The first had a more somber tone after the death of John Paul II: everything revolved around that. We were 115 cardinals, of whom only two had participated in the previous conclave. So we had no idea what to do; we spent the first days studying the apostolic constitution *Romano pontifici eligendo* with the help of the canonists who would answer our questions. Then the official nine-day mourning period introduced some problems that needed to be solved: Who would preside over the Masses celebrated during these nine days? And the funeral? When was the conclave to start? On the last day of the pre-conclave, on April 16, we celebrated Cardinal Ratzinger's birthday, and the next day the conclave began. To prepare ourselves, as cardinals we got together and we organized ourselves into groups according to continents to present a picture of the situation of the church in each continent. It was interesting, but we did not have much time.

But, in the last conclave, we had no pope to mourn. We only had to understand better, and together, what was working in the church and what was not, how to reform the economy after the IOR scandals, and how to reform the Curia. Regarding the latter, for example, Benedict XVI was not always well informed due to the "filters" that prevented the pope from receiving the right information.

We all shared many perplexities. There were also many divergences of opinion and different interpretations that sought to provide offhand explanations of the ecclesial crisis of that moment and Benedict's resignation. But in due course the strongest argument prevailed, because after the initial shock it became clear that Benedict's gesture had been a fully coherent act of faith. I personally admire his freedom of spirit.

# IV

# AND THEN CAME FRANCIS FROM THE END OF THE WORLD

*The Meeting with Bishop Bergoglio. A "Revolutionary Pope." The Revolution of the Gospel.*

*Did you know Jorge Mario Bergoglio before he was elected pope?*

As bishops of Latin America, we know each other well, because there is a continent-wide institution called CELAM, which I have already mentioned. The way it is organized and the style of communication between the various bishops' conferences are such that we interact frequently and with great familiarity.

In addition, as secretary general and then as president of CELAM, I was able to get to know all the bishops from all of the other countries and become familiar with the particular realities and pastoral dynamics of those different places. For this reason, I have been in close friendship with those who were bishops during my time as CELAM's leader and coordinator. Later, there were some special situations that allowed us to get to know each other even better.

Providence wanted us to work together—Bergoglio and I—in the commission that drafted the final document of the Fifth General Conference of Latin American Bishops at Aparecida, and there our friendship became even stronger.

I think that the familiarity between priests and bishops is a great asset. Friendship has always been regarded as a quality originating from Christian charity, and in the church it has always been considered a way of fulfilling our priestly vocation to consecrated celibacy and as an expression of that universality that brings with it chastity for the kingdom. I can assert that the best examples of holiness of life and the most beautiful testimonies of fidelity are those that I have found in these illustrious friends whom God has put in my path.

*If I am not wrong, you have often argued with Bergoglio as well—correct?*

No doubt. When our opinions would diverge, we would debate in all openness. Now he is the pope, and our relationship is inevitably different, but it has not affected our openness. And, besides, Bergoglio has changed a lot since he rose to the Chair of Peter. Before he was very austere, very reserved, but now he is like a father. It is a beautiful thing. I once saw him in Santa Marta laughing and playing with a child, the son of one of the kitchen staff.

I was sincerely impressed and amused, also because he loves children and young people. It is extraordinary the way he is able to imitate the Good Shepherd. He is a true pastor.

*What are your affinities? What are the things on which you agree?*

I never thought about it! Bergoglio is a man who loves the truth, who is not afraid to say things and call them by their name, without mincing words. And I like that very much, because I'm a bit like that as well. I also think of his great love for the Lord Jesus Christ. He is an example for me in terms of prayer. He gets up every day at 4:30 a.m. and, more or less, from 4:45 to 7:00 he is in prayer. He then celebrates Mass in the Chapel of Santa Marta, after which he greets one by one all the faithful who participated. Not only does he greet them, but he always has a few words to say to them, and at times he even takes pictures.

In these gestures he really is like a father. People are very excited to be around him. His first guests at these morning Masses were those working in the Vatican Gardens and the cleaning staff. He devoted the first year of his pontificate to them only. Since last year, people from the parish churches in Rome have attended his Mass, about eighty in all, as many as the chapel can accommodate.

And after a very busy day of work, Francis still finds time for an hour of prayer before the Blessed Sacrament, from 7 to 8 p.m. I wish I could do the same! But for now I cannot.

*Francis is called a "revolutionary pope." Do you agree with this definition? What is Bergoglio's revolution about?*

It is the revolution of the Gospel. He is not changing the doctrine, as some say—no. Our commission, for example, is not working on church reform but on the reform of the Vatican Curia. But we are also his advisers. And the pope has the right to call us when he wants us to ask for advice, even by phone. This is something that was unthinkable before. Now it is almost normal.

When he calls me on the phone, one of my two assistants answers. The pope now recognizes her voice and asks her immediately how she is doing. "Holy Father?" she says surprised. "Yes, yes, it's me; do not be afraid. How are you?" The revolution of the Gospel passes through a pastoral sense of closeness to the people, with great tenderness and especially with boundless mercy. I know of many cases, which I cannot mention here, that testify to his truly extraordinary heart.

I think that his revolution consists of a Christocentrism that manifests itself as a passion for suffering humanity, that part of humanity that is hurting and in need of love. All that follows comes from this fundamental option, and it is the fruit of a heart full of mercy and tenderness. The rest, I repeat, is nothing more than an irradiation of this inner fire that illuminates the mind and translates into words and then initiatives that revolutionize the world and that stirs in many people, even within the church, emotions and questions.

*What kind of relationship does Francis have with the Italian bishops?*

From the little that I know—good. The Italian Bishops' Conference is special because it is the only one in the world that does not elect its own president, who instead is nominated directly by the pope. Francis wants to change this tradition. Next year, when Cardinal Bagnasco will end his mandate, the Italian bishops will elect their own president.

Moreover, with regard to the appointment of the cardinals, Francis is following other criteria, because the cardinalate according to the current pontiff is not a way to reward a diocese, but rather it is a duty as the pope's advisor. Therefore, not all the historical dioceses and archdioceses, like that of Turin, will automatically see their bishops or archbishops become cardinals.

*Francis has said that he has never thought of resigning from the papacy. In your opinion, however, would this be a possibility that he might consider if he feels that he is losing his strength of mind and body?*

I think that the pope said this in answer to the many insinuations that have been made with regard to his coming eightieth birthday. On the basis of how the pope feels, however, he can continue to govern the church perfectly until he decides in conscience. Age itself is not a limit for the supreme pontiff. However, we must have a general picture of all the situations in order to decide if a person is still sufficiently able to carry out his mission in the church, in particular as pope. I think the pope is doing very well; I see him full of vitality, strength, and with great intellectual acumen and clarity. I often say that this bishop of Rome will be around for a long time.

# V

# FRANCIS'S DREAM

*A Church That "Goes Forth." A Church That Is*
*"Poor and for the Poor." A "Restless Church."*
*The Debate on* Amoris Laetitia.

*What does* Evangelii Gaudium *represent in Francis's pontificate?*

It is a bit about Pope Francis's plan for leading the church. It is his mission statement, just as other governments do: a new government begins and presents its most important programmatic goals. This is how I see it. Certainly, *Evangelii Gaudium* is a very pastoral document. The title itself is important. Francis often repeats that to be Christian is to be joyful. It reflects the joy of the Gospel. With *Evangelii Gaudium* and *Amoris Laetitia*, in their titles, the pope emphasizes that Christianity should not be depressing. There is, therefore, no church that thinks only for itself, a self-referential one, but a church that announces the joy of the Gospel and opens its arms to the world. Unfortunately, some people have not even read *Evangelii Gaudium*, at least not in its entirety. The same thing happened with *Amoris Laetitia*. As I have already said, *Evangelii Gaudium* is a great pastoral plan that presents us with different aspects of how to make Christ present, concrete, and alive today, not as just a historical memory. In this sense, there are some interesting passages in which Francis exhorts us not to be robbed of our missionary vocation. This is one of Francis's main points because the pope wants a church that "goes forth." Missionary activity is not an intellectual category, but life. It is a church that becomes—as in war time—a field hospital where the wounded are healed, where they also welcome those who are separated from the church for various reasons.

Moreover, *Evangelii Gaudium* warns us not to be robbed of our joy, our missionary enthusiasm, and above all the privileged attention to the poor, one of the points on which Francis, since the beginning of his pontificate, has insisted very much: "I want a church that is poor and for the poor." What can be more Salesian than that? Don Bosco wanted the Salesians to accompany the poorest of the poor and serve them: the first ones in Turin, today those from all over the world. This is another point dear to Francis—service as a sign of strength.

The pope, in the pages of *Evangelii Gaudium*, also pays attention to homiletics, a difficult theme for many priests. The Holy Father is almost offering a pastoral treatise on homiletics. There are priests who are well prepared for eucharistic preaching, others are not; I do not know where the faithful find the patience to deal with these priests and their impersonal homilies. And so the pope stresses homiletics as a crucial point in his pastoral program, the church's plan of government—and it is something that all priests must take seriously into account. This does not mean that one must read many books to prepare in the best possible way, but that the priest must pray more. This is the example I have received from Francis himself: looking at his daily routine, despite his many commitments, he manages to carve out daily an appropriate personal time for prayer in the morning and an hour of adoration in the evening before dinner. Therefore, his simple homilies at Santa Marta are homilies that come from the heart and prayer. These are words that leave a mark, deeply affecting those who listen! Francis is a contemplative of the Word.

Another aspect, again, is that of reform. In the interview released on January 22, 2017, to the Spanish newspaper *El País*, to the question whether Francis could be called a reformer or a revolutionary, the Holy Father replied no, that he is simply one who preaches the Gospel, and that a reform of the Roman Curia, of its structures, was necessary. Let's imagine a president who can only bring his ministers together once a year—that was the Curia. Pope Benedict XVI struggled to gather them once a year. At the pre-conclave congregations it was said that this was no longer possible, and that it was therefore necessary to reform the church to encourage collegiality. Many comment that although more than three years have passed since the creation of the "C9," there is still nothing that has been accomplished in this so-called reform. Thus, on December 18, 2016, the pope responded, in his address to the Roman Curia, listing and explaining the eighteen reforms so far realized.

Amoris Laetitia *is the subject of debate among critics and the most conservative Catholics. Why?*

For me, *Amoris Laetitia* represents the renewal of the pastoral care of families. It is a text that should be read and known by everyone, especially young people. When I meet couples preparing for marriage, I give them a copy of *Amoris Laetitia* right away: it is an aid to growth. For example, the fourth chapter comments on the hymn to love contained in the first letter of St. Paul to the Corinthians. For the meditation of couples it is very valuable. There is great enthusiasm among laypeople for *Amoris Laetitia* because they say it is a document that they read and understand. "When this pope speaks, we understand," people say, "while we did not understand the previous one; too much doctrine, too much theology. . . ." This is what we have to say to those theologians who, in reading Francis's words and texts, say: "This is not theology, this is a mess!" Evidently, they do not understand pastoral theology. Pope Francis, on the other hand, is a true pastor.

*There are some who say that* Amoris Laetitia *is not to be considered papal magisterium. Is that so?*

The cardinal who maintains this is a deluded man, because he wanted power and instead he lost it. He thought that he was the highest authority in the United States. As St. Therese of Lisieux once said, "I prefer to be small because if I happen to stumble, to fall, then the hit will not be so big; but those who are higher up make noise and hurt themselves badly when they fall." He is not the Magisterium; the Holy Father is the Magisterium, and it is he who teaches the whole church. The other just expresses his own ideas, which deserve no further comment. These are the words of a poor man.

*Amoris Laetitia* is a text of inestimable value. The reader immediately realizes that the language used is understandable; Francis teaches the doctrine of the church, but he does it with words that touch the heart, as did Jesus with the disciples at Emmaus. *Amoris Laetitia* is not a theological treatise, but it is Magisterium for families, to renew ties between spouses and generations. The entire exhortation is written in the pope's style—it is not the style of a theologian, but that of a pastor. Francis has reused many points from the synodal *relatio*, but he has also added so much of his own.

*In 2018 the synod on youth and vocations will be celebrated. What are your thoughts on that?*

For me it is great, though not unexpected, news because at the synod on the family we have suggested among the themes to face in the future precisely that of youth.

I recently wrote a letter to the rector major of the Salesians in which I expressed my joy because the synod will not only speak of youth in general, but of youth and faith—namely, vocational discernment. This is also a topic that is closely related to the synod on the family because, of course, there is a vocation to the priesthood, to consecrated life, but there is also a vocation to marriage and family life.

I reminded the rector major of the comment made at the 1994 Synod of Consecrated Life by the relator general, Cardinal Basil Hume, a Benedictine. He said that consecrated life was a theme *de re nostra agitur*—that is, "a matter of particular concern to us."

This is true of Salesians with the synod on young people, faith, and vocational discernment, because the Salesians are dedicated to young people and, therefore, this is a great challenge for the church and for our congregation.

My wish is that the entire Salesian congregation will allow a listening time, so that the preparation of the synod does not focus only on the *Lineamenta* promulgated by the Secretariat of the Synod itself. But above all, it is necessary to look at those difficult social realities of young people who are marginalized, distant, who never participate, or (I dare say) are gang members—even they have a voice. A great listening that can lead to a revitalization of youth ministry and of faith, one that is not simply transmitting knowledge or ideas from one head to another.

Faith is, above all, an attitude toward life. And when we have this attitude, young people understand that Jesus Christ wants to be their friend, someone who walks with them every day, especially in critical moments when they experience marginality and sin. I think this will be a great and beautiful prospect for pastoral outreach to youth and, especially for us Salesians, to return to vocational outreach.

Young people certainly have so many things to tell us, and we must be humble in accepting that we do not know everything and that we can still learn. When I talk to laypeople I learn so much; when I speak, for example, with members of the Academy of Sciences I know that I learn; even when I talk to young people I learn; I really enjoy talking to them because they teach us in their own way, but they always teach us something, and for me it's like being back at school.

*Today we see a decline in vocations to religious life and the priesthood. In your opinion, what are the causes?*

We have been waiting too long for young people to come to church. This is not the right attitude. We must go out, as Pope Francis told us in *Evangelii Gaudium*, to be a church that "goes forth." But you do not have to go who knows where; just the courtyard, the bar, at school, on the streets, in the oratory. . . .

Don Bosco recommended that we pay particular attention to those children who also have a slight prospect of becoming Salesians or priests. We must approach them, talk to them, become friends with them in order to guide them. I think that this is no longer done. There is almost a fear to make the vocational proposal. We must not be afraid of this.

I met so many magnificent laypeople in my country who told me: "I would have been a Salesian but nobody talked to me." And that makes me suffer. Why be afraid? Why are we ashamed to present our vocation, which is so beautiful? Hence, we need faith. I remember that at a pastoral meeting for young people in the United States—I was not present, but I read the acts— someone remarked: "We talk about Jesus Christ to the youth, but we do not teach them how to talk to Jesus Christ." This, to me, makes sense. It can be done with *lectio divina*, of which I am an enthusiast. If we bring *lectio divina* to young people, they begin to talk to Jesus and listen to Jesus. That is what is lacking, and then another horizon will open for vocational discernment.

*How effective can* lectio divina *be in the life of a young man who is in vocational discernment?*

When we were at CELAM we found out that this is a great way to bring people to the Word of God. In my country, since 1980, we have created a Bible fund to buy Bibles and sell them to people at a very low price. So many people have the Bible in their homes, but they do not read it because they do not understand it and because they were not taught *lectio divina*. So we started this program with a small foundation called "Ramón Pané." Ramón Pané was the first catechist in Santo Domingo. He was a lay catechist, and therefore we established this foundation with another layperson from Argentina. There are now many laypeople who devote themselves to this. For example, they can practice *lectio divina* on the computer with a program called *Cristo Nautas*, which is very useful.

When I was still president of CELAM, we put together a great educational program for young people through *lectio divina*. More than 80,000 young people on the continent participated. Truly amazing!

This theme is also close to my heart because I had a bad experience that made me suffer a lot. I was an apostolic administrator in a diocese in the western part of the country—Copan, which is very poor—and there was a lady who was always at Mass at the cathedral. I did not know her name, but she was always there. After a few months, I no longer saw her and I thought, "What could have happened? Maybe she's sick, maybe she's dead?" But one day I was walking down the street when I saw her, "Hello, how are you doing? I have not seen you at Mass recently." And she told me: "That's because I'm no longer Catholic; I'm Protestant!" "My goodness, what happened?" She replied: "Look, at the church where I am now we have the Bible; you celebrate only Mass." To me, that was painful. This lady was at Mass daily and did not understand that the readings were taken from the Bible. So I said to myself: if we lose so many people for the Bible, we are going to gain them back with the Bible, through *lectio divina*. We have to do it. The so-called evangelical churches have Sunday School, a School of God's Word. We, however, assume that the people already know the Word, and so we think homilies should be short. How much time do they have to read the Bible? So we also have to create schools of faith by loving the Word, and *lectio divina* is the best method to love Scripture. Once the young people understand this, they will not leave anymore. In Nicaragua there is a very poor diocese where they have nothing, but young people do *lectio divina* on their phones, and they send brief messages on the readings. It's a beautiful thing. I think that in this we Salesians must begin a revolution. How can we bring Jesus to the young through the Word of God and through *lectio divina*?

*How important is meditation in your daily prayer? Is it a practice for fellow priests and religious only, or is it for everybody?*

Absolutely. The people of God must be trained to practice meditation. How can the church, which has this treasure, not share it? But many laypeople practice meditation through yoga, and other Hindu practices, some travel. I know so many who travel from the United States to India to find who knows what, perhaps the secrets of well-being. They can do this in their parishes if the pastors have the creativity to teach meditation. I'm convinced that we can improve in this area and share it with people, with our laity. They need it, and when they learn it they feel happier and more free.

# VI

# "ÓSCAR, I NEED YOUR HELP"

## A Council of Cardinals to Help the Pope Reform the Roman Curia. Careerism in the Church.

*When did Francis call you to coordinate the council of the eight cardinals (who have now become nine)? How did you experience that?*

First, with great excitement, though we are good friends. We knew that once we elected the new pope, we could see him only by asking for an audience through the Prefecture of the Pontifical House. That day I was not well; my leg was hurting due to a fracture, but that phone call soothed my pain. I was in Rome, at the house of the ambassador of Honduras, where I was staying, and I received a phone call: "Who can call me from the Vatican?" It was Francis. "Holy Father!" I exclaimed. "Look, what are you doing on Sunday after the Angelus?" "Whatever you want me to, Your Holiness." "Come over for lunch, here at Santa Marta." I then asked myself: Why in the world would the pope invite me to lunch just four days after his election?

That lunch was wonderful, because before that I had only had dinner once with John Paul II and never with Benedict XVI, who almost never invited anybody for lunch because he is very frugal with meals.

During lunch, then, Francis said: "I thought I would create a council of cardinals with this person and that one and that one . . ." He already had all the names in his head. "Do you feel like coordinating the council?" "Well, Your Holiness," I say, "if you ask me, I'll have to." But that was not the only time we had lunch together. Sometimes I ask him for an audience and he tells me that he does not have time, so he invites me to have lunch with him. The last time was September 4, 2016, on the occasion of Mother Teresa of Calcutta's canonization. On these occasions we can talk openly. So many times he urges me: "Tell me clearly what they say is not working." Francis is a humble man. He does not want to hear only praises, but also criticisms.

*What criteria were used to choose the members of the pope's council?*

The criteria were mainly geographical. One from Oceania, one from Asia, one from Africa, one from Europe, while the Americas are different because they are like two continents, an English-speaking one and a Spanish one. Then the pope asked to include someone from the governorate, and later we asked him to include the secretary of state because he is the one who must implement the reforms and if he is not in the loop, he cannot do that. These were the main criteria.

*From being a son of Don Bosco, would you ever have thought that one day you would be close to the pope as an adviser? How do you live this role and how does this responsibility, given to you by the pope, influence your spiritual life?*

Of course not, to answer your first question; I would never have imagined it. I always thought of myself as a Salesian, so in my aspirations I felt already old, but always among the young, in class, teaching, directing a musical band, hearing confessions. I never thought of the episcopate as a possibility, much less of becoming cardinal. God's will led me to collaborate with the Holy Father. If I could have chosen my own path, I would not be what I am now, because my spiritual aspiration has always been to be a father and pastor for young people. But Don Bosco said that no task is difficult when it comes to helping the pope. It is with this spiritual attitude that I live my current responsibility.

*How is the reform of the Roman Curia proceeding?*

The first issue we have faced is the economic one: after two commissions (one on finance and one specifically on the IOR), the Secretariat for the Economy was born. Then it was time to reform some of the canons in the Code of Canon Law. Then we dedicated time to the communications issue with the new "super dicastery," which, for the first time, brings together all the Vatican media—a reform that will require at least three years to be fully implemented. It will reduce the Vatican Radio staff and produce a well-defined communication policy. We are also working on renewing the media sector because much of the equipment is now obsolete. We got rid of those very high antennas that are on top of the Vatican Radio building, which have caused litigations with the Italian state due to radiation. Further, they were shortwave antennas, which no country uses anymore.

There was also the reform of "Laity, Family, and Life" and of the Dicastery for the Integral Human Development Service, which includes "Cor unum," "Justice and Peace," "Pastoral Health," and "Migrant Pastoral Care." We are currently working on the nunciatures, the Secretariat of State, the Congregation of Bishops, as well as on culture and education. So there is still a lot on the agenda. Instead of writing the Constitution first, we decided to implement and start a change first. Official documents will be written only at the end of the reform. The council of cardinals is not just about reforming the Curia. Once the Constitution is drafted, it does not mean that the C9 will end. The council is permanent. Perhaps we will be replaced, because our mandate lasts only five years, but after that a new council will continue.

*After the appointment of a special apostolic commissioner to the Franciscan Friars of the Immaculate Conception and a special delegate to the Order of Malta, someone commented that the pope is anything but a man of mercy, as he wishes to appear, and that at his first opportunity, he exercised his sovereign power. Is that who Francis really is?*

Journalists write what they want. They do not know Francis. He is a true priest, not a man of power, but a Jesuit, and this is important because his spirituality is all about discernment. In this he is a son of St. Ignatius of Loyola, because St. Ignatius in his *Spiritual Exercises* insists on discernment, and that is what Francis seeks to accomplish every day. His job, first and foremost, has been to know the situation of every continent. He is a humble man who receives and accepts advice on everything: that's why he wants to hear directly from the different continents and that's why he has a special relationship with us. We do not go to the Apostolic Palace, but we meet in a room at Santa Marta. Our first meeting was at the Apostolic Palace, but when the meeting was over I told the Holy Father: "Why come here? It takes half an hour to get here, and half an hour to go back. Why don't we meet here at Santa Marta?" That same afternoon we were already gathered in the simpler setting of the Domus Sanctae Marthae.

The pope participates; he is with us all the time; and almost all the time he listens to us in silence, intervening every now and then, sometimes to ask us questions: What do you think of this, of that . . . ? It is beautiful to perceive his humble effort to understand and getting to know the situations. He also takes coffee with us. It's just wonderful.

For example, before him the pope never came to the meetings of the Synod Secretariat. Francis was the first pope to attend and there he stays from beginning to end, listening to what people say. Before, however, the pope never left the Apostolic Palace. Francis, on the contrary, is used to attending the Latin American Commission, to go to the optician, to the dentist . . . One time, after his visit to the dentist, he told his driver: "Take me to the

Latin American Commission," and the driver replied: "Your Holiness, there is no guard there," and Francis said, "I am the pope," and sitting beside the driver he was driven to the via della Conciliazione, where the meeting was taking place. He got out of the elevator, knocked on the door, and asked, "May I come in?"

It had never happened before. You could meet the Holy Father only in the Apostolic Palace, at an audience of no more than twenty minutes; and then if John Paul II would invite you to lunch, it would be a delight as you could stay up to two hours in conversation, telling some jokes as well. With Francis, I can say that we all feel relaxed and free to talk.

*How is Francis during the council's work? Does he listen and take notes? Does he often intervene or does he prefer to speak at the end?*

The presence of the Holy Father within the Council of the Nine is always very lively and hands-on. Our council is characterized by teamwork. Often, after having entrusted our work to the Lord, the Holy Father listens to the conclusions of the previous meeting, expresses his opinion, approves and cooperates by sharing his views, and finds his place in the working sessions as one of us. During breaks, he is very entertaining with his cordiality and good sense of humor.

His interventions are usually very terse; he prefers to listen. What is really admirable in him is his prodigious memory, capable of remembering every single detail; this allows him to have a profound, acute vision of both a particular reality and a general problem. Within the Council of the Nine, the Holy Father is really a great collaborator.

*It seems that the criteria with which the Holy Father chooses the new cardinals has changed. Is that true?*

There is a new mentality, as I mentioned earlier. First, cardinals were traditionally the bishops of specific dioceses. Pope Francis has changed that. The college of cardinals must include representatives from throughout the Catholic world. At the last conclave, there were sixty European cardinals, more than half the total, and Europe does not have even half of all Catholics. Some countries had never had a cardinal. In Central America, in Honduras, for example, I am the first cardinal. In Nicaragua there is already a second, while El Salvador has never had a cardinal. Panama now has its first cardinal. . . . This new arrangement is aimed at promoting a universal representation. That is why I told the pope that Australia is not Oceania. I came to know Oceania when I was president of Caritas Internationalis. There are some very poor countries who need representation. That is why Francis created the cardinal of Tonga, an archipelago in the Pacific; then another for New Zealand; and also one for the Papua New Guinea Islands. These bishops and cardinals are truly heroic men of the church. In Africa, Cape Verde has two bishops, one of whom is a cardinal. No doubt Europe is not happy about it: why did Francis not create a cardinal from Turin, choosing instead one from Chicago? Why did he not choose the patriarch of Venice? The pope wants all the people of God to be represented, even the poor of the smaller dioceses, to have a complete picture of the Catholic world in the United States as well. Today there is also a cardinal of Indianapolis, a diocese that has never had a cardinal, and now it has one.

Moreover, the pope is an extremely sensitive man. For this reason, he created cardinal a priest who was a prisoner under the dictatorship in Albania, and also Monsignor Renato Corti, whom I can say is truly a wonderful bishop. I'm glad that Francis has made him a cardinal.

*Compared to today, to what Pope Francis is already doing, how do you envision tomorrow's church?*

I think that this great impetus given by Pope Francis is above all to "go out," to be a church that "goes forth." In many places I saw clergy in their parish houses waiting for people to come to them; but people do not come anymore—we must go out to look for them, like Don Bosco. Don Bosco could have been happy in his clerical residence or with the Marchioness of Barolo; instead he went out looking for young people. Many Salesians have realized that street children and young people in the streets, those in gangs, need to be called and invited. We have a Salesian parish in Tegucigalpa, my city, which operates in the poorest neighborhood, surrounded by gangs. However, these youngsters, these delinquents, also respect our Salesians because they see them educating their younger siblings.

Once they invited me to launch a soccer tournament. They were kids, but the uniform was beautiful, all green with the words "Fifth Commandment: You Shall Not Kill" because the team's name was intended to teach the fifth commandment, since over there they're killing each other every day. So, I think that my confreres have come up with a beautiful initiative, a great idea.

We are very much appreciated when we are with the poor, but when we start to become more gentrified, then criticisms rage. We must always remember that our mission is to seek those who suffer from where they are, far from the church, wounded and in need of care. Certainly, several continents face widespread secularization—for example, in Europe—but sometimes it is because we are afraid to draw closer to others to tell them who Jesus is.

They told me an anecdote about the current archbishop of Turin. He invited young people to pray in a church, I think at nine in the evening, and when he arrived there were only two or three youngsters. He prayed with them and then left, a bit sad, only to pass in front of a shabby bar packed with youngsters, and so he went in. Yes, he went into the bar! Can one imagine a bishop entering a bar? After a great silence, he sat down and began talking to the youngsters there for two hours. He finally left full of enthusiasm. I was told that he also went into the next bar he came upon. We need more of this kind of witness. I see all these youngsters out there, and they need us. We must go to them without fear and without discouragement; no doubt we will sometimes get negative reactions but generally, young people appreciate priests who hang out with them and love them.

*What worries Francis these days?*

His greatest concern is, above all, to understand how priests, bishops, and cardinals can give greater witness to evangelical values. A small sign of witness can be seen in the simplicity of Francis's clothes. From the first day he was elected, he has not changed his wardrobe. Many have made a fuss about this. Someone asked, "Your Holiness, why do you wear those pants?" And Francis replied, "Why, what's wrong with them? Are they bad?" "No, but you can see them under the white robe." And the pope replied, "But they serve their purpose! When these pants are old, then I will look for a pair of white pants; now I'm fine with these. In fact," he added, "so they can see that the pope is the one who 'wears the pants.'"

Jokes aside, the pope is really worried about the witness to the Gospel and about the longing for power that continues to corrupt many members of the ecclesial body. When I and the other C9 cardinals had our first meeting in October 2013 (we counselors were appointed in April 2013), during the months of interregnum—that is, May, June, July, August, and September—each member produced his own "constitution" that he would then share with the C9 (I wrote a kind of new *Pastor Bonus*). The pope at the meeting tells us: "Well, excellent job, but our greatest problem is the economic transparency of the Vatican," that we would have to work first of all on the economic reform and that the IOR scandal was just the tip of the iceberg.

The IOR had become a real disaster, not out of malice, but due to the lack of a unified administrative vision. I can say without hesitation that every Vatican dicastery used to do everything on its own, separately; there was no budget, nothing . . . Can you imagine the madness of a state that never makes a budget in order to govern? We have reported various deficits, missing here and there, so we had to work on this issue at the meetings of October and December 2013, and in February 2014 we agreed to form a new dicastery, a sort of Finance Ministry of the Church. From there came the "cleaning up" at the IOR, which is not over yet. We must gradually integrate the common laws of the

European Union, adopting greater transparency and eliminating a lot of accounts that should not have existed in the first place. One case, just to give an example, is that of the monsignor who used his Vatican bank accounts to launder millions of euros.

*Like Don Bosco, even Pope Francis knows very well that a good example always goes far. What impact do his gestures have?*

Pope Francis's gestures, small and great, are incredible. One day, at the Santa Marta residence, I came out of the elevator and saw a ball rolling around and a child playing with the pope. He was the son of one of the employees working at Santa Marta's cafeteria, who had brought his wife and son to meet the pope.

I remember that at our first C9 meeting, when we went to Assisi at the end of a really tiring day, the pope had a great meeting with about forty thousand young people and answered almost all of their questions.

Another charitable gesture was toward the homeless. The homeless in Rome now have access to a barber at the Vatican; they have a place where they can eat, a place where they can take a shower and sleep. And let's not forget those refugee families the pope brought back with him to Rome when he went to Lesbos. These are gestures that speak to the heart and move people. They speak volumes. As Salesians, we must do the same. For example, Don Bosco would give away little medallions. Why can't we do the same today? It costs nothing. A holy image sometimes says so much to people, because people have a spiritual void that needs to be filled.

*When is the church not credible?*

When she says one thing but then does another. This was what the Lord said at the time of the Pharisees: "Do what they say; but do not do what they do," because the Pharisees would say one thing and then do the opposite. Our witness is extremely important; we must be coherent witnesses of what we teach. A good sermon that is followed by a bad example does no good. The ancients would say, *Verba volant, exempla manent*: Words fly away, examples remain. We must be coherent. We pronounce thundering homilies on charity and then end up being inattentive, incapable of listening, careless of our neighbors. Sometimes we behave as happened to me once, when I was a director of the seminary. There was a good professor who occasionally came to talk to me and used to complain because I always had a ready answer. He said to me, "Yes, Father, I understand, but consider it from this side . . . and that . . ." He was visibly uncomfortable. And he would go and complain to another Salesian: "The director does not listen to me; he does not let me talk." I understood that lesson, and I had to change and, thank God, I learned to say to him: "Of course, you are right. I have to listen to you until you finish what you want to tell me." We must have the patience to listen to our brothers and sisters, to listen to our young people; it is very important.

*Which "medicine" would you prescribe to those priests who do not live according to the Gospel, to whom people say: "You do not live as Pope Francis wants"?*

First of all, to not be afraid, because sometimes we men of the church are afraid. In a certain European country, not Italy, I have seen that to wear a priest's collar today means to be exposed to insults and even provocations. I have seen things that have made me suffer, like so many young people who no longer recognize priests and see them as odd creatures to shun or insult. That is why I say that these priests are right. But we can, nevertheless, do much more. Pope Francis, when he was a priest, visited the poorest and most disadvantaged neighborhoods. He was also insulted and indirectly attacked when there was the military dictatorship. I went through the same in my own country, though for political reasons, because I had denounced drug traffickers and they got back at me. But I have seen in Colombia an initiative that I liked very much: a group of priests asked for permission to put small confessionals in a mall, transforming one of these "cathedrals of consumerism" into a "cathedral of reconciliation." In the Year of Mercy, I found that more than ever people came to confession because the Year of Mercy touched them deeply. To see the Holy Father go to confession has done more good than many conferences on the sacrament of confession. Today we no longer need too many theories but gestures, and these gestures are important. To sit down with a purple stole in front of a church is a great sign.

Another charitable gesture that makes an impression is to visit poor families. I have done it myself many times, because most of my faithful are poor. When I go to the poorest neighborhood, people feel gratified because they think, "Ah! A cardinal who comes here, in my house, in this wretched place . . ." These are small gestures, I know, but people still love priests. In Italy, there is the tradition of blessing houses at Christmas. This rite is important; people are happy to welcome priests in their own home, and we must not be afraid. Some will say, "No, thank you!" And they will close the door on us. That's okay; they did the same with our Lord, with St. Joseph, and our Lady. But we need to persevere, perhaps even becoming more creative, for example, in how we invite young people. What Pope Francis did on February 14, 2014, left me stunned. We had a C9 meeting until Wednesday, and that Friday was February 14, and St. Peter's Square was packed. The pope had invited all the young couples to participate, and he spent time talking to them. These are beautiful initiatives; it's pastoral creativity. At times we lack this creativity, which Don Bosco teaches us, because he was an authentically creative man of his time.

*Francis has already condemned "careerism" in the church and often returns to the same topic. Has the pope ever thought of taking drastic measures against it?*

Yes, that was really a scandal. He also abolished the title of "monsignor." It makes no sense if it is just to wear a red or purple sash. Here, in the Vatican, there were so many, and the pope said, "All right; first finish what you are doing here and then go back to your diocese." Five years and that is it; this is part of the reform. You can be reappointed, but not for more than ten years in the Curia; then you go home because otherwise you will no longer find your place in your diocese, in your presbytery. You become an outsider who returns without a task for pastoral care. Why is this so? Often bishops would send some of their good-willed priests to serve in the Roman Curia, who, once there, do not want to return to their dioceses because they cannot wait to finally wear the purple sash. Francis said no to all of this. This is not the style of the church. You are in the Curia to serve, so it is a temporary position, not a way to make a career. This has created quite a stir and—I must say—a not-so-hidden hostility. I think that if the Holy Spirit has sent us this pope, it is obvious that this reform must be implemented. I think it is the right choice.

The Curia itself should help with the reform. It could not have gone any longer as it was before Francis's pontificate. The on-going consolidation of the dicasteries I think will help a lot. There is no need for so many cardinals in the Curia. The same goes for bishops. There could even be just priests, or even many more laypeople. We are working on this, to have more laypeople in the administration of the church. Why are we sick of clerical-ism, episcopalism, and cardinalism?

# VII

# ONLY THE GOSPEL IS REVOLUTIONARY

*The Denunciation of the "Throwaway Culture."*
*Attention to the Least Ones. Welcoming Immigrants.*

*Your Eminence, you have said that Francis's revolution is the*
*"Revolution of the Gospel." What does that mean in concrete terms?*

The true revolution is only in the encounter with Christ. What is the revolution of the Gospel? People's change of life—that is, their conversion. The true revolution is the conversion that begins when a person knows himself or herself, takes a close at himself or herself, and transforms his or her life in the spirit of the Beatitudes. Many times in our lives, we become victims of the idolatry of the I, of our egoism and selfishness. We think we are the center of the universe, while we are just a particle, albeit important, of a body called the world and a reality called the church. In this communal and universal horizon, I, as cardinal, am no more important than any layperson. We all contribute to the building up of society and of the Body of Christ.

We have to give an ethical and concrete answer to two basic questions: "Who am I?" And "What am I doing here?" Once believers, human beings, seize the essence of their identity, understand what their place is in the world as persons and the ultimate meaning of their lives, then they begin to live ethically. When people inflate their identity, they think that the whole universe should revolve around them, and with that come errors, depressions, greed, disorders of all kinds.

When we recognize who our Creator is and the greatness of Creation, then there is conversion; this is the true revolution of the Gospel. The true revolution is the one that comes from within, a conversion "in the flesh" that is realized in concrete practices and choices.

*What kind of relationship binds the pope to the poor? Those who live in the Vatican, how do they see Francis's concrete interest in the homeless?*

The pope has a special relationship with the poor. He helps them a lot. For example, I remember the case of a young man whom Bergoglio, as bishop of Buenos Aires, had helped so much. One time he came to see him here, and Francis said to him, "What are you doing here?" "I had to come and thank you for everything you did for me." And the pope asked him: "But how did you come to Italy?" because he knew that that young man did not even have a job. "I have a pilot friend who brought me here for free, keeping me in the cockpit. And that is how I'll return home, but I had to come and thank you." And this is just one of many people Bergoglio has helped. But the pope would want to do more if only time allowed it. He has a very busy schedule with numerous commitments, including trips, which for the pope are very demanding; he does not like to travel, but he understands that he must do it and he does.

I can imagine that some in the Vatican are not happy with the new style of this pontificate. The Vatican was almost a monarchy, and now for some people it is too dull. But we have to pay attention to the times we live in. Take cars, for example. That, too, is a precious witness. There's no need for luxury cars to go around in. Francis uses a Ford Focus, which is nothing special. Those two small Fiats he used in the United States were sold for a large sum of money to help the poor. These are little gestures, but they speak volumes to so many. Why not do the same? Each one of us, from all walks of life.

Today, it is not easy to assist the Holy Father in the Vatican, precisely because different people do not share his style and choices. As I understand it, I myself am not particularly liked within the Leonine Walls. But I don't care. I don't want anything; I don't lose anything. However, thanks to God, I also have many friends at the Vatican who appreciate and respect me, and with whom I work in perfect harmony.

*A cardinal told Bergoglio when he was elected pope that he should not forget the poor. How can the church be concretely close to the poor and, above all, to which poor?*

First of all, this is an expression that comes from the New Testament. When Paul and Barnabas visited Jerusalem, they gave the community pastoral recommendations: "Remember the poor" (Gal 2:10). From there comes the option for the poor.

The church has always been close to the poor in so many ways: fighting unjust poverty and against what Pope Francis calls the "throwaway culture," or against an economy that kills, because it is a profit-centered economy and not one that focuses on the dignity of people. Or when he speaks of a church that needs to give up so many things that are not necessary, of so many unnecessary luxuries. Of course, we must take care of our churches and give them dignity. But dignity does not mean luxury; luxury is not necessary, just as luxury cars are not necessary.

Francis asks us to give up the superfluous so we can share with others. This is very beautiful and good for us religious. We who do not have money, what can we share? We can share our time, what we know by instructing others, what we are passionate about. For example, I like to share my passion for music.

I can share my joy with people who are sad, find time to visit the sick that nobody visits, or prisoners. I have been twice to the prison near Malpensa Airport (Milan). I was invited there by the chaplain. There, I felt an enormous tenderness, because I have found many young people from Latin America who were deceived. They told them, "Take this package and we'll pay your trip to Italy." And so these youngsters came to Italy carrying drugs, but as soon as they landed in Malpensa they were arrested. I celebrated Mass with them and heard the confessions of some of them.

During the Jubilee of Mercy, I was able to enter a Honduran prison; before it was impossible because it was too dangerous. During that year, the entrance had become a Holy Door, after listening to Pope Francis who said that the door of a cell could also be a Holy Door.

We celebrated Mass and heard confessions. So many came that day. I also visited the women's prison, making a contribution to start a micro enterprise there so they can earn some money. Again, these are small, beautiful things that can be done.

Then there is the poverty of our young people who have no points of reference. Those who come to us are privileged. But how do you get to know those who do not come to church? This is the option for the poor. Education is the best recipe to overcome poverty. Without education, one has no chance of getting out of poverty and, therefore, we must do it without hesitation.

When I hear that some Salesians have given up being educators, I say, "That's not okay." Public schools are almost always worse because of the various ideologies or because of the professors, who are neither educators nor instructors and who do not primarily teach positive attitudes toward life, which are more important than all the various notions. For me, these are ways to overcome poverty.

*The church, Francis says, does not advance with organigrams but is guided by the Holy Spirit.*

As it has been said many times, the Holy Spirit is the great unknown. But the Holy Spirit is in action if we let him act, and he acts in all of us. Even nonbelievers can feel the Spirit. Sometimes people call it intuition. If I have faith, I say that it is certainly an intuition, but this intuition comes from Someone who leads me. And if I act according to that intuition, I am certainly doing what is good.

I strongly believe in the Holy Spirit: he is my ally in everything. I do nothing without invoking the Holy Spirit. Even before this interview, I prayed to the Holy Spirit: "Tell me what I must say." I've been doing this since my days as a student of theology when something significant happened.

I would study many hours and sometimes, when it was not allowed, I would get up with a companion at three o'clock in the morning to continue studying, without anybody knowing, until five o'clock. Around that time, and terribly hungry, we would eat a piece of bread the nuns of the kitchen would always leave for us.

One time, on the day of an exam, I was convinced I knew everything. But suddenly, I felt that I did not remember anything. Terrified, I prayed: "Lord, I understand that this is a way to humiliate me because I am conceited." But it didn't work.

Then I prayed to the Holy Spirit: "Have mercy on me!" And, as if by magic, I immediately remembered everything. From that moment, I do nothing without invoking the Holy Spirit: before a conference or a meeting, before preaching, before hearing confessions, before celebrating Mass or any other sacrament. Before I begin my lesson with my theology students, we call upon the Holy Spirit because he is the one who speaks and I am simply the spokesman. Always the Holy Spirit! Even Francis relies very much on discernment, and one cannot discern without the Holy Spirit. It is the Spirit who guides us, and we must let ourselves be guided by the Spirit.

*Pope Francis often speaks of a "bruised" church or the church as a "field hospital." How do you imagine the church?*

There are so many wounded people, many people who wander away from the church—thinking that the church is only a rigid institution, where everything is defined, everything is said; that there is no place for those wounded by life, or wounded by some members of the church, or by some laypeople who think they are perfect. I do not want to refer to anybody in particular, but there are some movements that almost adhere to a sectarian ecclesiology, along the lines of "Here we welcome only those who are already on the right track; all others may leave." That is wrong!

Don Bosco clearly had the right attitude. There was certainly the oratory, but he would go out, in the streets of Turin, to the building sites to find bricklayers, carpenters, day workers who toiled to earn a few pennies a day. He wanted to instruct them and teach them a craft. Then, he would go to the villages, with joy and with a band, and would entertain everybody to attract young people, especially those who were far away and did not understand anything about the church. Don Bosco was looking for them, and then he would bring them to the oratory, letting them play, and then he taught them the life of Jesus. This is the type of "hospital" we need.

Just think of the children of the divorced, who are wounded people. When I was a priest in Guatemala, I worked a lot at the center for family integration, because there was so much social disintegration, and that starts when there is divorce. Divorce, which now seems to be a fashion, is instead a failure; in Spanish we say a *fracaso*. It is the failure of a union that is meant to be forever. When people get married, they say "forever." And the children, instead, are often wounded. They do not know what to do. They are left without an identity. Even a small plant needs a little bit of earth to bloom. They, however, have no home because a weekend is spent with their dad, another weekend with their mom. Then they have to deal with their mom's boyfriend and father's girlfriend, and the disorientation only increases. All this creates enormous suffering in young people and has consequences even after they become adults: they do not want to marry to avoid making the same mistake as their parents. These are very serious problems that the recent synod has tried to address. Unfortunately, we have only discussed whether communion should be given to people who are divorced and remarried, but all these other issues on how to help divorced couples with their children is our job as well. This is a "field hospital," a hospital to heal wounds. Just think of those who grow up without their dad, many sons and daughters of single mothers, children whose dad was just an episode in their lives. It is an even bigger problem in my Latin America, where the majority of young people come from single moms. What are we going to do with them? How can we help them heal? How to help them see life in another perspective?

Then there is another issue we face when a pastor, a shepherd of souls, does not have the right pastoral attitude and sends people away by doing stupid things. So many people turn away from the church because of a rude remark from a priest. We must be kind to heal these people.

I, more than ever, have understood with Pope Francis that being a pastor has a "medical" dimension. It means being a doctor of souls, a doctor who heals. And this healing happens especially when we have Jesus in our heart; only then can we bring Him to others.

*Regarding migrants in Europe, the pope has said that the Mediterranean becomes a cemetery of people who reach our coasts already dead. Do you think Italy is doing much in the rescue effort?*

One of the points we discussed at the C9 was precisely the reality of immigration. When we consolidated the dicasteries of "Justice and Peace," "Cor Unum," "Migrants," and "Health Care" into a single large dicastery, the name we chose to give it is appropriate: "Integral Human Development." What does this remind us of fifty years after Paul VI's encyclical *Populorum Progressio*? Francis told us that for the time being he himself will head this dicastery's section dedicated to migrants.

There have always been migrants in the world. Migration is a human right, but now, the situation is very serious, especially because of wars and economic underdevelopment in many countries.

Italy is doing a lot. Just look at what happened in Calais: What we saw there is that the great nation of France is not really sympathetic to migrants. There are several things to do. First of all, we have to look for the cause of this situation. And the cause is a terrible war—fighting in Syria has been going on for more than five years. And what does the world do? Look the other way! The United Nations should express a unanimous and immediate condemnation, saying: "Enough! Let's stop this war!" But then coordinated action would be needed, as well as an international strategy.

The same happened in the Balkans, in the former Yugoslavia, in the 1990s: when in the former Yugoslavia different ethnicities were killing each other. Why? Because Russia and the United States were interested in selling weapons. War instruments serve the war economy, revitalizing the economy of the major arms-producing countries, mainly the United States. And the economic crises are solved because the factories are producing what kills people.

For Putin, however, it is a matter of power. He was accustomed to being the great "Emperor." Then his prestige diminished and he wanted to restore it. How? With this war, unfortunately. This war needs to be stopped; this way many would not be forced to migrate.

The same thing happened with Libya. They killed Muammar Gaddafi who, though a tyrant, managed to maintain peace among the various tribes. The mistake was to impose a democratic system in countries that are not yet prepared for democracy. The tribes, in fact, continue to fight and people continue to flee from wars.

These are the mistakes of the United States. Then there is ISIS. Finally, something is being done against ISIS, which is financed by Saudi Arabia, a great friend of the United States. If they wanted it, ISIS would disappear tomorrow. But war is more lucrative. And so many refugees, so many illegal immigrants flee to Europe to survive. What is left for them in their own country? Nothing! They have nothing to lose, so they migrate. And then there is the attitude of countries like Germany, Greece, and France—a deeply rooted phobia. This must end.

We are facing a "piecemeal" world war, as Francis said. Unfortunately, we never learn anything from history. The twentieth century saw the bloodiest wars in history. And now we are in a full piecemeal third world war. There is that dictator in North Korea who even has atomic weapons. What does he think he will achieve? By triggering a war, he would be the first to go down. And then there is China, which is currently the most powerful country, stronger than the United States.

*What have you learned from the church, the Salesians, and the poor?*

The poor are always a school of life. In my city, which is the see of the archdiocese, there are so many places of extreme poverty. There are juvenile criminal gangs in Central America, the famous *maras*. It all originated from some Salvadoran immigrants in Los Angeles. From the Salesians I learned that when we assist the poor, they respond with great loyalty and love. In our parish, we are surrounded by criminal gangs, but since the Salesians educate their little siblings, they respect the Salesians, and there is no danger.

I administered the sacrament of confirmation in many parishes, but I remember that one time, going to a parish, at some point I was stopped by the police who warned me not to take a certain route because there was a criminal gang in that area. But they never disrespect us. In the poorest areas we have two schools, and there they respect the Salesians.

I recall that Fr. Egidio Viganò, the rector major of the Salesians elected in 1977, always warned us of becoming too "middle class." If as Salesians we abandon the low-income neighborhoods, if we abandon the oratories, then we go wrong. I think the oratory remains a brilliant idea and the winning card to achieve good results in difficult neighborhoods. It does not matter the country or culture: the oratory remains a value that must not be abandoned. To drop a word in somebody's ear, as Don Bosco would do with his kids, is not out of fashion. We must continue on this path because this is a Marian pedagogy; our Lady inspired this pedagogy.

*What is your experience of poverty and chastity?*

Poverty, for me, has never been a problem. Actually, since my novitiate, I have always felt good with the little I used to have and still have. I never had any problems because if I wanted something, I would ask for it. If it was given to me, okay; if not, it was the same. I must say that because of our lifestyle, which was quite secluded while I was studying philosophy, we were not so tempted by excessive consumerism, and even less so during the period of aspirantship. And the same goes for the period of theological studies. In short, I've never had any problems with poverty.

As far as chastity is concerned, however, there was, of course, this energy that I felt within myself, but it was not that difficult to handle. Ours was a very clean, healthy environment . . . of friendship, joy, and prudence. As a priest, I sometimes had problems when some women approached me not with the desire to seek spiritual advice, but with other types of desires. In that sense, I once had a bad experience with a woman who wanted me to hear her confession, but in a separate room, and I told her no, that I would hear her confession in the confessional. But she replied, "No, I prefer your office." All right. I noticed, however, that this woman had other intentions. Another time, I was visiting a sick woman's home and that same woman was there also because she was a friend of the sick lady and I did not know that. I was there to hear the sick lady's confession and after doing so, the other woman arrived and asked me, "Can you hear my confession?" What could I do? The woman came in but instead of confessing, she gave me a hug, and she also wanted to kiss me. I said, "Madam, please, I am a man of God. You are about to desecrate a sacrament. We cannot perform the sacrament of reconciliation here. I want this to stop, especially in front of your friend who is sick. So please put yourself over there and pray and ask for the Lord's forgiveness for what you wanted to do." She stayed there a few minutes, and after that she left and since then I have not seen her again.

Sometimes these things happen; we have a heart and we can fall in love. It is quite natural. And what do I do when I fall in love? I distance myself. This is the only solution. I do not say that it is easy, but it is not too difficult either. I remember that when my first nephew was born—I became his godfather because my brother had asked me—while baptizing him, I thought to myself, "I, too, could have a son." But then the Lord gives me other children.

*What did you learn during the years when you were president of Caritas Internationalis?*

Caritas is in 164 countries in the world, and this is a great blessing for the church. Many people think that Caritas Internationalis exists only for emergencies. That is reductive. Caritas is, first and foremost, a great communal service, a school of social doctrine in the church for all churches, and I must say that the Italian Caritas is one of the best in the world. But in some countries, Caritas is considered only an agency to obtain money to fund projects, and that, I assure you, is not its main purpose. It is first and foremost a school of Christian sharing of goods. I learned, in the years of my presidency, how love is really the engine that moves people, because *caritas* is love—a concrete love, made of concrete gestures—but it is also a school. So many people think that Caritas Internationalis is only an NGO, and that is incorrect. It is church in action; it is education for the Christian communion of goods. Caritas is a school—a training school to learn how to share, a training school for a Christian communion of goods—that teaches us that even the poor have something to share, that nobody is so poor that he or she has nothing to give, and that nobody is so rich that he or she has nothing to receive and is never in need. Even the rich can receive faith and joy when volunteering, for example.

I knew a young man, son of a very wealthy family in my country, his parents were about to divorce and he led them through *lectio divina* to understand that their marriage was a lifelong union. They were reconciled and did not divorce, and this young man, a young professional, grateful to the Lord for this grace, devoted a year of his life to missionary work in a poor parish, leaving everything behind. He came to me and asked me to go to the poorest parish of the diocese. I sent him there and in one year he did amazing things. Then he returned home to his family and resumed his job. These are beautiful things, and I am convinced that even the rich have this possibility. This is *caritas*. Caritas Internationalis is present in over 160 countries. Even in Russia, Syria, Iran . . . even amidst all the difficulties. In Morocco, for example, the staff is all Muslim; only the director is Christian, but everything works just fine. I think that this is an important lesson and that Caritas Internationalis should be at work not only in emergencies, as I said. We also have programs for the promotion of women's rights; we have programs to fight AIDS; we have educational programs on the church's social doctrine. It covers a very wide spectrum. It is wonderful to see how the church is engaged in charity work.

*So is there also salvation for the rich?*

Absolutely; salvation means sharing. And when they understand this, the gates of God's heart are wide open. I know so many cases of rich people who are happy because they share and serve others. One of the great entrepreneurs in my country, who is a very rich man, has created a cooperative for all his employees. Now everyone has a decent home; everyone has a decent salary and lives a happy life. This man has never seen a strike, and his workers have never protested because he has always looked after them and shared with them. So his business is also thriving. This has nothing to do with the wild capitalism that the pope has denounced. That is in the hands of truly greedy individuals who want to accumulate more and more, and never share anything. This is a terrible and difficult disease to cure. But, yes, the rich who do good and share with the poor are on the path of salvation.

# VIII

# "NOT WALLS, BUT BRIDGES"

*The Persecuted Churches. Other Christian Confessions.*
*Dialogue as a Method In and Outside the Church.*

*Regarding the persecutions in the Middle East, what can the church do and what should it avoid in order not to exacerbate further threats from terrorists?*

I believe that the church is doing what it ought to do: accommodate refugees. At the end of my appointment to Caritas Internationalis, I visited refugee camps in Jordan; they live in desperate conditions. The church must continue what it is doing: the works of mercy. What the church did and continues to do is urge the leaders of powerful countries to look at this situation and not turn a blind eye.

The trip to Lesbos was a great effort for the pope, but he did it with a strong determination to become a witness, as if to say, "You have to do the same."

He washed the feet of twelve poor refugees, all Muslims; he did not choose Catholics—these are signs that speak volumes. A Protestant friend wrote to me, "Congratulations on the pope's encyclical." I replied, "What are you talking about? The Holy Father has not yet published any encyclical." And he caught me off-guard, answering, "I am referring to the encyclical of his gestures," those gestures that Francis performs every day. I remember that one time, when the pope went to Sibari, in southern Italy, in a small car. Among the Calabrian people in the street, he saw a disabled girl. He had the driver stop the car, got out, and went toward her; he kissed her, blessed her, and then continued his trip. You would have never seen that happen with previous popes. Another time he left the Vatican to go to the optical store for a new pair of glasses. These are gestures that form the "encyclicals of gestures." That optician will never forget that experience, ever.

*How can the church build bridges with the world?*

No doubt with dialogue, because the church was created for dialogue. When Paul VI's pontificate began, I was a young Salesian, and I remember I was expecting with great curiosity his first encyclical, *Ecclesiam Suam*, published in 1964, which focused on dialogue. I read it, and at first I wondered if at that moment in the church there were no more urgent issues to be addressed than to write about dialogue in the church. . . . Some years later, as a student of theology, I admit that I was sorry to have had that critical attitude toward Paul VI's first encyclical.

As a young Salesian, I was very rebellious. During the years of my formation, I experienced the transition from the pre- to the postconciliar period: I completed my novitiate and my studies of philosophy before Vatican II, so all in Latin; then my apprenticeship during the council and my studies of theology were after the conclusion of that great event for the church. I had a huge crisis, because I realized that until then I had thought that certain things were fundamental, indispensable, and instead they weren't at all. From that moment on, I realized that dialogue was a methodological priority for the church. I think Paul VI was inspired by the Holy Spirit in thinking of that encyclical. Without dialogue, the postconciliar period would not have been possible.

Prior to Vatican II, the Salesian congregation had about 23,000 Salesians, while after that the number dropped to 16,000, and afterward we were no longer able to reach that number. Before Vatican II, in my Salesian province, we were almost 400

Salesians, and we were already thinking of dividing it into two, there were so many of us. Then, after the council, there were less than 200. I say this not because I believe that the council was the cause, but I think it brought to light many vocations that were not profoundly motivated.

But, returning to "dialogue," I firmly believe, even more today than in the past, that it is the church's path and that we must continue to build it with the world, without excluding anyone.

*Is ecumenism making headway with Francis?*

We have already experienced important moments for ecumenical renewal. Credit also goes to Patriarch Bartholomew, the most Catholic of all Orthodox leaders, who has great respect and appreciation for Pope Francis, as does Francis for him. The Lesbos initiative was his idea. His was a real stroke of genius.

Let's hope in other similar gestures—for example, a possible encounter with the Patriarch of Moscow.

*Do you have memories of your experience as bishop with other Christian confessions?*

During the three years of preparation for the Jubilee of 2000, the year of Christ was the first year; then came the year of the Father and the year of the Holy Spirit; and finally the fourth year, the Jubilee, was the year of the Trinity.

We were in a commission to prepare for the year 1997, and the lay associates organized a series of initiatives. One of them suggested: "Here in this city we have no monument of Christ, nothing; why not put a big cross on the mountain?" And I said, "Not a bad idea." The following month, at another meeting, they came already with the project of a risen Christ, and I said to myself, "Where will I get the money for this?" However, the third month they had already found an architect who was willing to complete the task. I was impressed by the entire project;

it was beautiful, a beautiful risen Christ, ten stories tall, that is thirty-two meters. . . . I talked to the president of the republic about that monument and he said to me, "I can give you that land; part of that mountain is national property and we can donate it for this project"; and then he invited his ministers and me to lunch. I explained the idea of making a monument of the risen Christ and then establishing a foundation for all those poor people living there in the mountains, in miserable homes: Let us provide them with worthy homes while reforesting the mountain. The project was a great success. The president said, "I will donate one month of my salary for this project and I invite my ministers to do the same." Only two of them eventually did, but with that money we started the work and, finally, when the year of Christ ended we inaugurated the monument. This was in Honduras. Evangelical Protestants railed against us, saying, "This is idolatry; fire will come down from heaven to destroy everything; we will destroy that monument." But when on the day of the inauguration I invited an Orthodox priest, who was in the city of San Pedro Sula, and the Episcopalian bishop, who eventually came, it was beautiful.

Later, in 2007, with a politician and an old student of mine, we started an ecumenical commission. We had a very good ecumenical dialogue, even with evangelicals, but misunderstandings started when *Dominus Iesus* came out, because they began to criticize it. Then I asked, "First of all, please tell me: who of you has read *Dominus Iesus*? Nobody. And how can you criticize it without knowing it? Let us meet again when you have read Pope Benedict XVI's statement!" It ended all there, unfortunately, because these Pentecostal churches generally say that ecumenism is from the devil, not from God. These are just some of the most unfortunate episodes, but I recall a very beautiful one as well.

Some time ago, in Germany, I was visiting a family in Heidelberg, and Ascension Thursday was coming, and the Lutheran pastor came to invite me to concelebrate a service of the Word with him, and I went. It was wonderful. So, we are making some steps in the right direction, but Latin America is still behind when it comes to concrete ecumenical progress, and not only in words. These evangelical churches have very little religious culture, so it is difficult to establish an ecumenical dialogue with them. But I can recall a few funny anecdotes as well. For example, when Pope Francis visited the primate of the Church of England, the encounter was friendly and fraternal. The primate at a certain point asked the pope: "Do you know the difference between a liturgist and a terrorist?" The pope had no clue and did not know what to say. "The difference," the primate said, "is that with a terrorist at least you can negotiate." And they burst into laughter.

*With which continent today does the church need to be more in dialogue?*

With Asia especially, because 60 percent of the world's population lives in Asia and there is not a significant presence of Jesus there. I'm not talking of the church, but of Jesus, who is not known there. If we remove from the picture the Philippines and South Korea, in Japan and elsewhere Christians make up 0.1 percent of the population. Indonesia is the most Muslim country in the world. Therefore, Asia is truly to be evangelized. How? The Holy Father is concerned about it, and for this reason he will visit India and Bangladesh. These are important gestures. He has already visited South Korea and the Philippines.

Then comes Africa, which is the continent where there has been rapid growth of Christianity, especially of Catholics, and there is a flowering of vocations. Latin America, however, is at a halt, and growth has stopped.

I think that today, the Holy Father is the most respected leader in the world. Not because Francis is a genius or, I don't know, an academic . . . no, but because you can tell that he is a man of great moral stature.

# IX

# THE MESSAGE OF MERCY

*The Extraordinary Jubilee of Mercy. The Holy Doors of the World. The Fruits of the Jubilee.*

*What message did you convey to the prisoners you visited in Honduras?*

I especially insisted on hope. "You," I said, "are not meant to be in jail for a lifetime. You are here because you made a mistake. But one mistake can be corrected and paid for. You are here to find a new attitude toward life that brings you to better things."

Some of them have killed; many do not even understand the value of life—among them, gang members. I met a boy who at the age of fifteen had already killed five people. How to make amends for this tragic and partly unintentional mistake? Some youngsters are already so affected by drugs and crime that I think it is very difficult to rehabilitate them. Some should go to a psychiatric center, but in Honduras we do not have one for young people. Yes, there are two neuropsychiatric hospitals, but they are really horrible. Placing a young man in jail and condemning him to life in prison is a disaster. This is a social crime that is repeated in so many places in the world. But what do you do with these young people when they leave prison? To sustain hope is very important for them.

In prison, I also met many illegal migrants. In Honduras most of our youth want to leave for the United States, thinking that they will find the "Promised Land" there. Sure thing, now that President Donald Trump wants to build a wall . . . truly unbelievable in the twenty-first century. Just horrible.

*Did you feel the need to live a year dedicated to God's Mercy?*

From the beginning, I realized that Pope Francis had the theme of mercy in mind, but when the Jubilee news came out, I said, "Yes, the Lord really considered it necessary." The Holy Door and confessions have meant a great deal to our people. On Holy Thursday, at the chrism Mass, all of us priests and the two bishops went to the Holy Door in front of the crowd to show that we also need God's mercy, and this is a great message to the world. So many people have come to confession after years and years without the sacrament.

When we hear the confessions of the faithful we realize how great is the need for a special grace like this. When we are aware of the existential drama of so many people who feel excluded, who are wounded, who suffer from the consequences of insurmountable poverty; when we open our eyes to perceive the truth of the imbalance in the world, we understand that an Extraordinary Jubilee of Mercy was urgent, fundamental, and indisputable. And the Holy Father wanted it and got it done. May the Lord bless him!

*Did you expect Francis to launch an Extraordinary Jubilee?*

The Holy Father is an extremely independent man. It is amazing and enchanting to witness his prophetic way of doing things, and his various gestures are truly "encyclicals" made with firmness and clarity. His gestures, expressions, symbolic actions, and interpretations of society and man are in harmony with mercy. That mercy is what he wanted to emphasize and that he wants to make known to the world as God's attribute; that mercy of which man is the object and at the same time a continuator and propagator.

To be honest, the announcement of the Extraordinary Jubilee of Mercy by the Holy Father was not a complete novelty, but—as I have already said—I was surprised and moved, noting that Pope Francis does not sleep or rest until he achieves his goal. And to give to the whole world the great wealth of God's merciful love was truly a gesture of astonishing generosity.

*What were the visible fruits of the Holy Year of Mercy in your opinion?*

The visible and palpable fruits of the Extraordinary Jubilee of Mercy are so many. In the diocese of Tegucigalpa, and throughout Honduras, there have been thousands of people who daily crossed the Holy Doors designated to obtain the plenary indulgence; and these people did it in faithfulness, with due preparation and with the awareness of doing it as a paschal sign. All this has renewed and increased in parishes the fervor of the priests and the faithful, who pray and attend with more assiduity. Other tangible fruits are the works of corporal and spiritual mercy: many Christians, individually and others as a family, have been engaged in their parishes or diocesan communities in admirable initiatives, performing various works of mercy. This is something that is contagious, which is inspiring an engaging atmosphere of enthusiasm and commitment to "do mercy" in all its manifestations and expressions. For many people, it has become now more clear that when we ask forgiveness for our omissions at the beginning of Mass in the penitential act, we are not referring to a matter of moral order but, more concretely, to charity, compassion, solidarity, and mercy toward the other.

# X

# WHO IS NOT MERCIFUL TO FRANCIS?

*Resistance to Reform. Conservative Catholics.*
*Toward Greater Collegiality in the Church.*
*The Theology of the Papacy.*

*Who is not merciful to Pope Francis? For what do they not forgive him?*

I would not know, because he is merciful to everyone. I am a witness of how Francis helped a lot of priests with problems, how he especially has helped the victims of sexual abuse by the clergy. This kind of concern, which is also part of the reform of the Curia, now under the attention of the Commission for the Protection of Minors, is not simply to deal with cases of abuse, but of prevention; the pope has met with victims many times and some of the victims are members of that same commission. The first day that this commission met, there were two ladies, very somber looking, sitting at a table at Santa Marta having breakfast, and I felt sorry and thought that I would go and sit with them. They did not talk to me. So I introduced myself and then asked the first of the two who she was, and she replied, "I am one of the victims of an Irish priest when I was a little girl." Then, luckily, the ice was broken. Recently, the commission faced difficulty for the resignation of some of its members citing reluctance and resistance. It takes a lot of patience.

Another person who has not been merciful to Francis is Venezuela's president, Nicolás Maduro. One day he had said horrible things on the radio against the Holy Father, claiming that Francis, while being Argentinian, is playing in the hands of the United States and this is something that Venezuela cannot tolerate; Venezuela must be respected. Then Maduro mentioned Cardinal Enrique Porras for his fascist attitudes, "and we'll see if we'll keep him as our cardinal." This is what he said on the radio. Then Maduro came to the Vatican for a meeting with Francis. An unplanned visit. Maduro was in Saudi Arabia for OPEC, the Organization of the Petroleum Exporting Countries, and made his way to Rome to come, unexpectedly, to the Vatican. The pope welcomed him all the same. But Francis is frank and he told him what he thought.

*How could two Italian journalists be charged in the "Vatileaks 2" trial?*

When it comes to human freedom, we sometimes find ourselves facing unexpected surprises. Each person is a world in itself, and in the world many things can happen. Therefore, that two Italian journalists were implicated in the Vatileaks 2 process can be explained by the fact that in every human heart there is always room for weeds to grow along with the wheat. There is no doubt that many of the biggest breaches of trust come from people who are most close and trusted by superiors.

*Francis has been attacked by "conservative" Catholics on several occasions. A recent instance was when he opened a discussion on the diaconate for women. Do you think there is a possibility of new roles for women in the church? Is a study (even at the liturgical level) to find new forms of service for women in the Catholic Church really necessary?*

The resistance to Pope Francis by some groups and some "conservative" currents are the result of simple prejudice. What the pope said about the diaconate for women was not pronounced in academic and magisterial terms. He simply said that we need to study the possibility, even when we know that this is a topic dealt with in the history of the church several times. The female diaconate was, among other things, accepted and widespread in Christianity in the early centuries. I think the pope leaves doors open for new forms of diaconate, for new ministries and specific services, in which women can develop their feminine genius and express their ability to serve, always characterized by fidelity and generosity. The ecclesiastical tradition did not recognize the element of female discipleship with the same significance as it did with the following of Christ by men, even though in the Gospel it is said that the apostles were with Jesus "as well as some women." Jesus allowed a group of women to "follow him and provide for him" (Luke 8:1-3; 23:49; Mark 15:41).

Luke places male and female disciples on the same level, on equal terms of commitment and fidelity, since they both follow Jesus closely. In his Gospel, Luke also handed us the names of some of these disciples: Mary Magdalene, from Magdala, who had been healed from seven demons; Joanna, the wife of Chuza, governor of Galilee; Susanna; and some others. It is said of them that they "provided for them out of their resources" (Luke 8:3). They, therefore, carried out a concrete and effective *diaconia.*

When the Gospel of Mark tells us the details of Jesus' crucifixion, he writes that "there were also women looking on from a distance." Among them Mary Magdalene, Mary, the mother of James the younger and Joses, and Salome. They used to follow him and "provided for him" when Jesus was in Galilee. Along with them there were "many other women who had come up with him to Jerusalem" (Mark 15:40-41).

Recently, the pope wrote a letter about the laity in the church, in which he states that neither men nor women should be clericalized.

When the pope raised the liturgical celebration of Mary Magdalene to the rank of solemnity, he also did so with the intention of highlighting the special mission of this holy "apostle," an exemplary model of every woman's commitment to the church.

*In a report published by the newspaper* La Stampa, *journalists Andrea Tornielli and Giacomo Galeazzi presented the "universe of dissent from Pope Francis." There is, in fact, much of the Catholic right, with important names, that criticizes the pope at every opportunity. How should one consider these oppositions: Should they be relativized or listened to? In particular, is it right that they exist in the first place?*

No doubt, we live in a pluralistic world. However, if these are baptized people, it means that they are lacking in faith. I can disagree on something with Francis, but he is Peter's successor, and if we have faith, we believe that this is the pope whom the Lord chose. I can say this openly. I cannot speak for the conclave from the inside, but it was clear there that this was the pope whom the Lord wanted.

In other words, I cannot speak of the various discussions during the conclave, but there were certainly other undercurrents, and some even very strong because they had already been lobbied for. At the end of the day, the other "papabili" cardinals, whom others wanted to elect, lost while the one the Lord wanted was elected. Dissent is logical and understandable; we cannot all think in the same way. But it is Peter who guides the church and, therefore, if we have faith, we must respect the choices and style of this pope who came from the far side of the world. These attacks from the Catholic right are from people who seek power and not the truth, and the truth is the only important thing. If they speak of finding some "heresy" in Francis's words, they are badly mistaken, because they are seeing things from a human point of view and not from God's.

I think that a quality for us cardinals must be loyalty, and even though we do not all think the same way, we must, however, be loyal to Peter and, in the case of the C9, to be the forthright advisers of the Holy Father. If I have some disagreement, I communicate it directly to him. What is the point, though, to publish articles against the pope, which do not harm him, but ordinary people? What can a conservative faction, immovable on some issues, do? Nothing! It just keeps the people away, and the simple people are with the pope; that is evident. This is what I see everywhere. The simple people are with the pope. Those who, on the other hand, are proud and arrogant believe they have a higher intellect. . . poor little men! Even pride is a form of poverty. The biggest problem, however, I repeat, is the disorientation that it creates in people when they read the statements of bishops and cardinals against the Holy Father. Again, I believe that for a servant of the church what is indispensable is loyalty to Peter, who today goes by the name of Francis. Before him, we had Benedict XVI, and before Benedict there was John Paul II, and so on. What Jesus asks of me is to be loyal to Peter. Those who do not act this way seek only popularity.

*They have accused Francis of going to Lund to commemorate the 500 years of the Lutheran Reformation, neglecting, in their view, an anniversary more relevant for Catholics as the anniversary of Mary's apparitions in Fatima.*

I'm glad for that. Glad because these are the brave gestures of Pope Francis, gestures that were and still are necessary. Why? Because he is the pontiff. What does "pontiff" mean? He is the one who builds bridges, and he cannot wait for others to do it in his place. Francis did precisely that, for example, when he embraced Patriarch Kirill of Moscow, something that was impossible before, but he did it! He did the same with Muslim leaders: we all remember, in the Central African Republic, when the imam, not a bishop, was riding in the popemobile with the pope. They are very important gestures, and Francis has this courage to take the initiative. So many have come to him, but for a pope to go to them is a gesture of courage and love; it attests to the will to take seriously the Lord's desire *ut unum sint*— that is, "that they may be one." This desire cannot be achieved if the pope sits in his Apostolic Palace waiting for others to come to him. This is something that Francis has understood very well, and so he puts it into practice. For me, this is very important. I am glad because it is a step forward. It is not a search for unity at all costs, but a way to take steps in the right direction—but steps that are credible and not just words, because ecumenism cannot be realized in words, discussions, documents, but only with gestures of sharing in the faith. For this reason, criticism is unacceptable to me. How can Francis be accused of not being devoted to our Lady when there is no trip where he goes without bringing flowers to the Mother of God and when he returns does the same? Francis is a wonderful Marian pope, and to make comparisons such as whether he marks the five hundredth anniversary of the Reformation or the hundredth anniversary of Fatima reveals small minds that cannot see beyond the strict parameters in which they are enclosed: they are imprisoned by ideologies. No, the pope is extremely devoted to the Mother of God, and he is also extremely ecumenical. What happened in Lund was a great gesture of utter beauty.

*Many see him as the antithesis of Benedict XVI.*

That is a big mistake. Every pope has a certain charism, a vocation, and offers his contribution to the church. John Paul II has left us an extraordinary magisterium with numerous encyclicals and post-synodal exhortations. He was a teacher, but he was primarily a missionary, and this cannot be forgotten. Pope Benedict XVI was a professor of theology and gave us precious teachings. Francis instead is a pastor, a shepherd who is bringing back many people to the church thanks to his pastoral attitude. It is not a good idea to make comparisons, because everyone is as the Lord wanted and how the Lord called each one of us. We cannot think that all popes must be alike. After Francis, another will come who will be different from him. We must be adaptable to the whims of the Holy Spirit.

Francis, perhaps, is not a systematic theologian, of course—he is not overly academic—but in what he says there is plenty of theology. What is theology? It is God. When, for example, Francis talks about the church and collegiality, he is doing ecclesiology. Every time he speaks of Christ, he is doing Christology. He is not developing theological theses, but he is putting theology at the service of the poor, a theology accessible to the people. In all respects, it is theology. And theology is not mechanics, it is not physics, it is not chemistry . . . it is theology. The pope is not elected to be a professor of theology; he is elected to be Peter, to be the guide of the church. And that's what Francis does.

*Pope Francis, some argue, seems to want to reduce the power and centrality of the figure of the Roman pontiff by giving more power to the bishops. Is it really so?*

I do not think Pope Francis is of that opinion, but it is clear that he spoke about collegiality at the commemoration of the fiftieth anniversary of the Synod of Bishops. That shows the great genius of the pope. Before, the church saw herself as a triangle: the pope, the Curia, and the bishops. Instead, with Francis, the Curia is at the service of the pope and also at the service of the bishops. There is still a great resistance to this new configuration, especially in the Curia. The Curia was in fact almost a super-structure over the bishops and the bishops were the sheep. That is no longer the case. This is a new style that cuts the strings of power in the church, with more collegiality, with more involvement of bishops and dioceses. The biggest obstacle is power. The greatest temptation in man—more than money, more than sex—is power, and power is hard to give up. So, the reform is going in this direction. Certainly, Pope Francis has very clear ideas and knows well the damage inflicted by the curialists.

# XI

# THE GOSPEL ON THE INTERNET

*Evangelizing in the Digital Era. Two Popes on Social Media. Priests and Nuns on the Web.*

*Your Eminence, you have been a member of the Pontifical Council for Social Communications and founder of Tegucigalpa TV. Is evangelizing on the internet a marketing strategy to "promote" Christianity, or is the web an environment where the Holy Spirit sends us to meet the men and women of this day and age with their thirst for spirituality?*

Very interesting question. Certainly, evangelizing on the internet is also a "marketing strategy," but it is not just that. If that were the case, it would simply be the use of the network as a tool, and in fact one thing is technology, another is the personal relationship between people, with all those vital, almost magnetic, networks that are generated around it.

The first thing the church did at Pentecost was to openly proclaim the Gospel. The first speech of the apostle Peter (Acts 2:14-36) triggered the immediate conversion of thousands of Jews. It is interesting to consider what was the effect of that first preaching: "Now when they heard this, they were cut to the heart and said to Peter and to the other apostles, 'Brothers, what should we do?' Peter said to them, 'Repent, and be baptized every one of you in the name of Jesus Christ so that your sins may be forgiven; and you will receive the gift of the Holy Spirit'" (Acts 2:37-38).

It is amazing to note that that first preaching of the Gospel pushed those who listened to seek a solution that comes from Christ. That is the focal point. We are not messengers of bad news but of salvation. We do not only speak about Christ, but rather propose an encounter, a personal exchange, an experience with him.

I am sure that St. Paul, who worked as a tentmaker, did that because it was the craft he learned. That type of occupation has practically disappeared, but today he would undoubtedly be interested in learning computer science to make it a field worth exploring, working for the kingdom, and operating through networks "whether the time is favorable or unfavorable" (2 Tim 4:2) to evangelize. The web offers enough incentives and alternatives to create a new culture through different Catholic sites, while offering new counseling centers for spiritual, sentimental, psychiatric, and physical well-being, or opportunities to discuss aspects regarding the major issues of contemporary society from a Christian perspective.

*Is the church called to educate the new digital generations, or is it not her responsibility?*

I have recently heard that there is psychological research, especially in neurology, and recent studies that show that exposure to the web and the computer world can alter the development of fundamental psychological processes such as attention, perception, language, memory, socialization, and learning—up to the very configuration of neural networks and the brain. And this takes place over a generation's time. The evangelizing mission on the internet begins with the evangelization of the network itself, so that it facilitates and guarantees a new way of transmitting values and living standards by elevating them to the highest level of humanization.

I believe that the education and socialization of the so-called digital generation represent for the church an immense responsibility, and we, the "digital nomads," must look for itineraries for these men and women who have spiritual aspirations and want to know the truth about man and God.

In Honduras, we are making great efforts; there is still much left to do—at times, it seems to me that this immense enterprise is comparable to a Sisyphean task—but with the passion for the kingdom, we will overcome all obstacles.

*What are the limits of the web in promoting a serious evangelization?*

The limits from the point of view of coverage, immediacy, simultaneity, and versatility are fewer and fewer. Actually, this is a phenomenon that is unifying and transforming humanity. It is true that the evangelization of culture and missionary activity may contribute to the in-depth growth of a fairer, more united, more just and friendly world, as a true instrument in the service of communion. *Aetatis Novae* is right when it states: "Nowhere today are people untouched by the impact of media upon religious and moral attitudes, political and social systems, and education."

Thus, there is no limit in yearning for what is good, especially if it is to defend humanity, proclaim the justice of the kingdom, and favor the reconciliation among people. The limiting of links depends on self-censorship, the principle of respect for diversity, the level of tolerance, and the ability to discern what can be done to avoid evil and to prevent the absence of moral standards to prevail, as well as the destruction of values such as order, truth, family, sacredness of human life, interculturality, and so on.

I believe that the boundaries of the web begin and end with the beginning and the end of the humanization process of the person. Therefore, it is a question that remains unresolved, a process that is in progress, and part of a constantly evolving reality. Where there are people, there is a need to evangelize. Talking about limits is like talking about containment dams, walls, and gulfs; but God, as Psalm 147:15 says, "sends out his command to the earth; / his word runs swiftly," which is to say that God's message runs and spreads with such vitality that it will always encounter limits to overcome and spaces that need to be Christianized.

Evangelization is not a way to express oneself through media, with this or that resource (from the pulpits of the past to digital TV), but a proposal for all cultures and is realized through dialogue and respect for all, until the Gospel is first assimilated, then integrated, and finally is expressed through that culture.

*Do people also seek God on the internet?*

The thirst for God (Ps 4:2) accompanies human existence as a tension and a vocation to what is transcendent, divine, and absolute. Nothing can satisfy this "thirst for infinity" because it is a necessity of fullness and happiness that defines the pilgrim man (*homo viator*).

It is only natural that people desperately look for satisfying answers to their "thirst for God" and that in the absence of answers, they try to fill this deep feeling by consuming "spiritual" by-products from whatever source they come from. Even what is religious, what is spiritual, has become trivial and offerings multiply with fascinating products, whether brand-named or not. There is no doubt that the thirst for God, which seeks to satiate a religious need, is growing in a way that is directly proportional to the eroticization of consumerism, hedonism, materialism, and absolute relativism.

The web can be a wonderful "platform" to introduce to the very life of the church—a kind of public window through which people are kindly invited to look a little more closely in the church, even just out of curiosity and even if they have some prejudice against it. The phenomenon of communication is an "Areopagus" that has opened up wide horizons that are full of novelty with regard to communicative activity. It is a wonderful "agora" in which we discuss and "compare the prices" and the quality of economic, political, cultural, social, and religious elements. In this way, even what is religious does not escape this dynamic of "classification" and socialization. A store window, an entrance, an Aeropagus—the important thing is to let people come in and become interested in Christ's message.

I believe that if we look at the web and its ample, complex, and instantaneous dynamism as a new missionary field, we must prepare people for it instead of waiting for the experts to jump in; rather, we need to encourage those who are inexperienced to come on board. If St. Paul's motto was "woe to me if I do not proclaim the gospel!" (1 Cor 9:16), then this might be a call for us to evangelize "the web" through social networks: Woe to me if I do not evangelize the web!

*How can a serious evangelization on the internet be accomplished?*

Since it is the church's task to announce the truth about man and God and to teach the Gospel to all peoples, the church does so with all the resources and means available. It is undeniable that social media has an ever-greater influence in determining new trends in social behavior and in defining a new cultural model. Among these, the use of the internet also offers a wide range of products and by-products of science, art, education, leisure, and sport, as well as many trivialities. Everything begins with a click that answers the questions of the user. Social networks and digital tools have unquestionably empowered the globalization of culture and determined new styles of behavior for young people, families, and emerging societies.

For this reason, in the pastoral instruction *Aetatis Novae*, the then–Pontifical Council for Social Communications stated that "the first Areopagus of the modern age is the world of communications which is unifying humanity and turning it into what is known as a 'global village.' The means of social communications have become so important as to be for many the chief means of information and education, of guidance and inspiration in their behavior as individuals, families and within society at large."

To do evangelization on the internet, I think you have to stick to a flight plan (sorry, but you know that I am an airplane nerd). Yes. I mean, you need to know where you want to go, how much luggage you can carry, and where we're taking our aircraft. It cannot be a naive effort; you have to remember who you want to reach, what message you want to communicate, what level of personal depth you want to make an impact on, and how long we have to be there to reinvent ourselves or to start over with new strategies, not proselytizing ones, but those of humanization and evangelization.

*First we had Benedict XVI on Twitter, and now Francis is also on Telegram and Instagram, along with the monthly videos for the Apostleship of Prayer. Is it to be trendy, or is there another reason that justifies this Holy Father's presence on social media?*

I think that it is in continuity and in harmony with a contemporary style intended to animate and encourage faith in those who speak a new language and who are part of a new era and intercultural dialogue. The last two popes knew how to benefit from the potentialities of the web as a great instrument for proclaiming the Gospel, convinced that this is a fascinating field. Consistent with this belief, they worked with determination to be part of the new media culture.

Benedict XVI expressed this concept in the inaugural address of the Fifth General Conference of the Latin American Episcopate at Aparecida, and he was very direct in this regard: "In this area, we must not limit ourselves solely to homilies, lectures, Bible courses or theology courses, but we must have recourse also to the communications media: press, radio and television, websites, forums and many other methods for effectively communicating the message of Christ to a large number of people."

I think that these are brave and coherent steps. I think they are in harmony with the universalization called for by the Gospel and correspond to the demands and needs of an interconnected society, which interacts in this way and whose communicative processes reflect the technology and means available.

I often think that Jesus did not use microphones or megaphones simply because they were not available in his days. Today, however, he would use these technological means as tools in the service of the kingdom that he had come to establish. In fact, the pontiffs, in accordance with the times, have been able to make use of these means to make themselves known where the people are. The one hundred thousand "likes" that a pope's message receives on Twitter, for example, demonstrate the strength that his message has in the vast and wide world that is the internet.

*Many religious, priests, and nuns . . . we cannot assume that they always make use of social networks in a responsible manner, perhaps because as novices and seminarians nobody taught them?*

In my experience, I have seen, in different parts of the world, more and more religious, priests, seminarians, and young people in training houses use social networks with familiarity and regularity. Reducing internet usage seems to me to impose an inadmissible "digital exclusion." We need to educate and lead in a positive way; this way religious, priests, and seminarians can deepen their understanding of a missionary methodology through means of communication and networks in an active and constructive way, without fear or repression. In addition, the internet and everything that comes from it is a means of evangelizing, not an end. It is a constant battle to know how to make the most of both the initial and permanent formation, so that the church's consecrated men and women and its pastoral ministers are prepared to face the challenges that technological innovations constantly require. We need to teach in view of not only a pastoral plan for communication, but also a communication for pastoral care, in the sense of transmitting life—and life in abundance—through social networks.

It is true: religious, priests, and nuns do not always make responsible use of social media.

I think that there has been an oversight in their initial formation, especially for those we call "digital nomads" (admitting also that some have "drowned" in the digital world); so the "dive" into the world of social networks—and the caution it entails—has been so different that for many it is still unbelievable.

No doubt, the impact of the "novelty" effect has passed and the reality of social media has sunk in, even in convents and seminaries. For this reason, the church's guidelines in the field of initial and permanent formation for the institutes of religious and consecrated life and seminaries encourage their positive use, even because the wealth of the ICTs (information and communication technologies) are by now an integral part of our everyday life.

Yet, looking a little further, say two decades from now, I wonder: How to survive in a sensitive and intelligent way in an increasingly global and complex environment? The digital phenomenon we are witnessing has no precedent, so we have no previous experience to fall back on; plus, we do not have enough time for exhaustive considerations, detailed analysis, and weighted and meditated decisions. I think that it is time not only for reflection, but also to make choices, come up with decisions, and implement them.

Lightning Source UK Ltd.
Milton Keynes UK
UKHW02f2022220518
323030UK00009B/545/P

9 780814 644027